Hey Guys, Did I Miss Anything?

A Journey Back, and Stories from Five Months in a Coma

This book, and my recovery, is dedicated to my support team of friends and family. You are amazing. To the healthcare workers who did everything to save my life. And especially to my family: my brother Taylor — you're the best brother and friend a man could have — and my incredible parents — without you, I wouldn't have had a chance. You are my rock.

Table of Contents

FOREWORD
Taylor Raborn, PhD

Nothing about the evening of September 22nd, 2011 betrayed the horror that it would later reveal. My brother David, four years my junior at 25, was preparing to ride his bicycle amid the beautiful late autumn weather in Alberta. Sitting at my desk half a continent away in Iowa City, Iowa, I received photos on my iPhone from David of the fall foliage outside his house near Sherwood Park, Alberta, Canada, then of his bike, whose handlebars he had wrapped with a colourful new pattern. I spoke with David minutes before he would set out for a bike ride. I was standing on the sidelines of a grass field, getting ready to play an intramural flag football game. Moments after the game ended, I opened my gym bag to check my phone. A single message appeared on my screen, from our mother: "David's been hurt. He fell off his bike. Please call." Frantic, I called just as David was being placed into the ambulance. During his bike ride, David had fallen over his handlebars after catching his tire in a pothole, hitting his head and fracturing his skull. My mother pressed the phone to his lips, exhorting him to say something to me. He faintly grunted, "I love you, Taylor" before his voice faded and he slipped into unconsciousness.

I don't remember much about the next hours except for the profound sadness and terror I felt at the looming possibility of losing David. My eyes moist with tears, I stayed up in my apartment maintaining contact with our father through the multiple brain surgeries, all the while gripped with a cold and numb sense of foreboding. While David made it through that night, his prognosis was dim. At his bedside in the Neuro ICU,

i

David's pastor had administered his Last Rites. Less than 36 hours after his accident, I was at the Cedar Rapids Airport at daybreak, bound for Edmonton. Shortly after takeoff, I gazed down at the cornfields below and began to write David's eulogy on an airplane napkin.

The events that would follow—encompassing anguish, sorrow, pain, hope, recovery, and love—make up a story that needs to be shared. You will read of a true community— friends, colleagues, and former teammates and classmates— uniting in support of a fallen loved one and his family. You'll read about two Good Samaritans: a minor hockey goaltender and his father who were running late to a Midget AAA hockey tryout, yet who stopped to help a disoriented cyclist on the side of the rural road they were driving along. You will learn about a university football quarterback who would travel from the practice field to the hospital to sit at his friend's bedside and give his friend's mother some needed rest, and you'll learn about the gift that David's perseverance gave him. You'll hear about a close-knit group of friends from high school who banded together after the accident to create "Team David" and "Beards for Broborn" T-shirts, and who built a Facebook group to share triumphs and setbacks. You will hear about the severity of David's brain injury, and how perilous his fate was, from the neurosurgeon who did the operations. David's astonishing rehabilitation at the Glenrose Hospital will be documented by those who watched David take his first steps after five long months. You will hear from these perspectives, and many others, to hear about David's truly remarkable recovery, and the equally remarkable demonstrations of love and sacrifice from the community that accompanied it.

Nearly four years to the day after David's terrible accident, my beautiful wife and I were married. Our wedding reception was held less than a kilometre from the University of Alberta Hospital where David spent many months in a coma. David was the best man. After he left the room in tears of laughter during his toast, recounting to those in attendance about the items I had to wear to a baseball game in Miami during my bachelor party, it was my turn to talk. I nearly brought out the old napkin where I sketched out the beginnings of his eulogy that cold late September morning, but at the last minute I thought better of it. I think that old napkin has been lost in a recent move, and it's for the best: our David is here to stay.

INTRODUCTION
David Raborn, B. Comm

September 22nd, 2011. I try not to let that date define me, but, more often than not, it does. The journey that I've been through since that Thursday evening has molded me into someone different. I believe it's made me stronger in many ways. The way I trust God and His plan for me has been strengthened. It has made me truly thankful for each day. I believe God has turned this negative into something extraordinarily positive. My bicycle accident brought many people together for the purpose of saving and nurturing one life. My life.

Many people, churches, and schools all around this world prayed. They wrote letters. There were countless hospital visits. There were so many visitors that two of my amazing friends hosted a magnificent Thanksgiving dinner for them all, in the hospital. (What I'm trying to find out is why they didn't invite me out to partake in this glorious spread!)

In all seriousness, it was quite the feast. How could such a tragic event turn into a beautiful, joyous party? I believe only God knows the answer to that question. I also believe He has plans for me. This book is part of His plan. Could this comeback story change the hearts of people who see it and read it to follow the Light of the World, the One True God, Jesus Christ? My pastor told my parents that he witnessed a couple of my friends come to Christ as they saw my situation and how it was unfolding. If even one person is saved through the reading of this book, then His work has been completed through my recovery. The significance of prayer in turning things around, especially for me, is undeniable.

I'd also like to stress the importance of wearing your helmet while riding your bike. Had I not been wearing my helmet, I wouldn't have made it to the hospital, let alone had a chance to recover. The doctors at the U of A Hospital told my family this. I also want to emphasize the importance of a supportive community of friends and family, if possible, around the injured person.

I wanted to showcase some of the most important figures of this story. Since I was taking a snooze at the time, I'm not a great source of information for the story. I get my facts from those who were so instrumental to my survival. The idea is to see the story and many of the "stories within the main story" through *their* eyes. I'm more eager than anyone to read this book and "hear" what they have to say about the most difficult challenge I've had to face in my life.

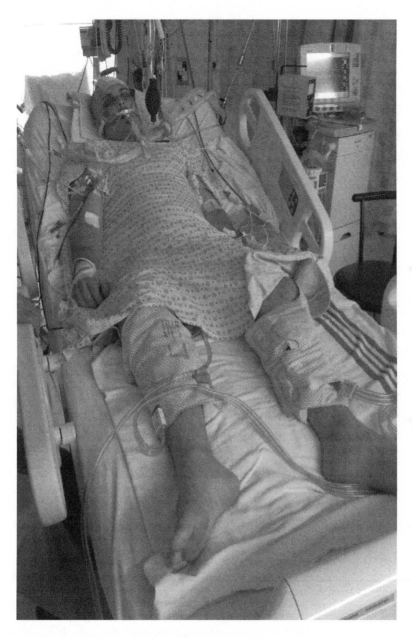

In the hospital bed, post-surgery

1. *BACK FROM THE BRINK*
Dr. Michael Chow

It happened on a warm Thursday evening in late September 2011, an evening that was perfect for a bike ride with the looming spectre of another long cold Edmonton winter on the horizon. This was going to be one of the last idyllic weekends of the rapidly fading summer and as the on-call neurosurgeon, I sensed that it was potentially going to be a busy night for head trauma.

Around 10:00 PM I received a call on my pager. It was the emergency room physician at the Grey Nuns Hospital. A 25-year-old patient, David, had arrived in their hospital after having been thrown off his bike. He initially was conscious after EMS brought him in but was becoming progressively comatose during his assessment in the ER. An emergent CT scan of the head showed a large right acute subdural hematoma. A large blood clot had developed between the surface of the brain and the dura, the membrane that surrounds the brain.

Fortunately, I was able to view the CT from my home computer and saw the hematoma with its significant mass effect. The brain was shifted from right to left due to the hematoma, and uncal herniation was present. In other words, the temporal lobe of the brain was starting to compress the side of the brainstem. One of the clinical indicators of this compression is a dilated and unreactive pupil on the side of the hematoma. It was clear to me that if left untreated, this would rapidly and inevitably lead to David's death.

Measures to temporize the acutely increased intracranial pressure were instituted. A rapid infusion of intravenous mannitol was ordered and the patient was intubated for transport to the University of Alberta Hospital. I had heard that David's right pupil was starting to dilate and lose its reaction to light. Once a neurosurgeon hears that the pupil is affected, it truly becomes a neurosurgical emergency. The brain is not a particularly resilient organ and is very sensitive to compression. It is not uncommon for a patient to remain in a perpetual coma or even progress to brain death if the brainstem is compressed for more than one hour. Time is *critical*.

The fact that David had presented to a peripheral hospital and had to be transported across the city to the neurosurgical trauma centre posed a significant obstacle for timely definitive treatment. It is all too common to have significant delays in "hand-over" of patients as they travel from one emergency room to another. To make sure this was minimized as much as humanly possible, I decided to come in to the University Hospital as soon as I received the call, prior to David's arrival. I spoke with the triage nurse in the emergency room to advise her that the EMS crew transporting David would bypass the ER and go straight to the operating theatre. Furthermore, I organized the operating room theatre so that the anesthesia team and nursing staff would be set up and ready to go as soon as David arrived. These simple acts probably saved at least 30 minutes of delay.

When David arrived, a brief clinical exam revealed that he had in fact developed a fixed and dilated right pupil. Within

2

minutes we had him positioned on the operating room table and were ready to begin our operation. A standard trauma flap on the right side of his skull with a generous cranial window exposed the source of his rapid deterioration: an extensive gelatinous solidified blood clot was removed from the surface of the brain, allowing the brain the resume its normal healthy pulsations. It was also quite apparent that the brain had started to swell, probably secondary to the contusions or bruising located beneath the surface of the brain. To address this problem, we decided to leave the cranial bone flap off, allowing the brain to swell out through the opening.

Once the operation was complete and the head dressing was on, I checked the pupil. A successful decompression is always accompanied by a return of the pupil to its normal size, and we were all relieved when this was observed in David. However, the story did not end there. Several hours later, early in the morning the next day, the same pupil dilated again. A stat CT scan revealed that another blood clot had re-accumulated in the space between the brain and the skin flap covering it. As well, the temporal lobe hematoma had increased in size. Once more, this created enough mass effect that the brainstem was compressed again, leading to the recurrent pupillary dilation.

We rushed David back to the operating room to evacuate this post-operative hematoma and further widen the cranial bony opening to allow for the anticipated brain swelling. Furthermore, we entered into the right temporal lobe to remove much of the newly developed hematoma. Thankfully, his signs of brainstem compression were alleviated with this second operation and his pupil returned to its normal size. We had "saved" David a second time! He was still in a coma in those early days and weeks, in our intensive care unit. As with most severely head injured patients in a prolonged coma, he underwent a tracheostomy and gastrostomy tube insertion, which both facilitated his eventual transfer to the neurosurgical ward. The support David received from both family and friends was extraordinary, yet I knew all too well that does not guarantee a significant improvement in a patient's recovery.

The improvement we saw in David was slow and incremental in that first month. The brain swelling had subsided and he was now left with a depression on the right side of his head where the cranial bone flap had been left off. I decided to replace the bone flap two months after his first two operations. The situation was complicated by the fact that David had developed a deep venous thrombosis in his left leg. This required anticoagulation, which was unsafe in the setting of a cranial operation.

We stopped his anticoagulation temporarily and the initial bone flap replacement surgery went smoothly as planned. We decided to cautiously restart his anti-coagulation a few days after this uncomplicated surgery but unfortunately, David had yet another complication of a post-op hematoma. This required his fourth cranial operation to evacuate the hematoma. Fortunately, David was not as severely affected with this post-op complication and it provided a relatively minor setback to his recovery.

A full five months later, David's journey to a remarkable recovery ended its chapter at the University Hospital and the setting moved to the Glenrose Rehabilitation Hospital. David celebrated his 26th birthday with us and the next day was transferred to the Glenrose. When he left us, he was still unable to verbalize but his responses were becoming more and more appropriate. The prognosis for his recovery was certainly still guarded.

There is no question that these multiple operations were life-saving. With the initial operation, if there had been a delay of even half an hour or less, David may not have recovered from his initial severe head injury. If the injury had occurred outside of Edmonton, I can honestly say that he probably would not have survived. However, over time, all neurosurgeons develop some degree of cynicism as to how "successful" these operations are. All too often, we see patients who are left "vegetative" in that they are awake but not able to interact with their surroundings. This puts in perspective David's remarkable recovery, which will be detailed later in this book.

As neurosurgeons, we have trained ourselves to remain emotionally detached when it comes to patient outcomes. Frequently, we see young patients struck down in the prime of their lives due to trauma. When we are fortunate to be able to save a life, we are just "doing our job". Nevertheless, I can honestly say that David's amazing and inspiring recovery has touched me deeply. As you will read in the following chapters, many people have been instrumental in David's recovery, but I am glad that I could provide my small contribution.

2. THE OCCUPATIONAL THERAPISTS OUTLOOK
Don Simoneau, *Glenrose Hospital OT*

I first met David in February 2012. He was 26 years old. He was an unusual patient for the Glenrose Rehab Hospital (GRH) as he had been injured five months previously in September of 2011 and had been in acute care for all that time. Most patients who come to the Adult Brain Injury Program have been injured weeks or perhaps a couple of months prior to entering rehab. Less frequently, like David, patients will come to the GRH after needing acute care for several months. Requiring this length of time after injury suggested to me that his injury was extremely severe and the odds of him recovering significantly were probably not great. Nevertheless, his journey in rehab would begin and time would tell how he would do. We would begin treating David with an open mind and see how he responded. Every patient's journey is unique, and after being an occupational therapist in a tertiary rehab hospital for 25 years, I've seen patients do much better than expected and, unfortunately, much worse as well; not every story has a happy ending. When David contacted me, hoping that I would contribute to a book he was putting together of his story, his voicemail message began with, "Hi, this is David Raborn. I don't know if you remember me; I was a patient of yours almost five years ago..." I have seen hundreds of patients in my career; some I remember and some I do not. That's the truth of it. With some patients, you develop a relationship and have an emotional attachment for whatever reason, and you'll probably remember them forever, whereas other patients are, quite frankly, difficult to recall after a year has gone by.

With David, I recognized his voice and knew who he was with the first two words he spoke.

Of course I remember you, David.

I first get to meet a patient by reading their medical history. I knew David was a single man, 26 years old who despite doing all the right things by wearing a helmet, had been seriously injured riding his bike. He most likely hit a pothole and went over the handlebars, striking his head on the ground. I say "most likely" because the accident was not witnessed. A passerby arrived after the fact and found David having had an obvious bike accident, bloodied and confused, with a badly damaged helmet. Emergency Medical Services found David also confused and worsening rapidly. At the emergency room, David was found to have multiple facial and skull fractures, bleeding on and in the brain, which was causing extreme pressure, leading to an emergency procedure being done where a part of his skull was removed to allow the brain to swell with less danger. Had this procedure not been done, David would have certainly died from his injuries. The social history read that David was a recent graduate of the University of Calgary with a finance degree, and he was a serious athlete playing university football with the Calgary Dinos. It was clear that this was a self-motivated young man with everything going for him up to the time of his accident.

There are different ways to grade the severity of a brain injury. The most common method we use at the GRH is the length of time a patient spends in the Post Traumatic Amnesia state (PTA). This is the length of time between when the patient is injured and the time that they start forming consistent memories of day-to-day events. A PTA of one to seven days in considered a severe brain injury. A very severe brain injury is any time beyond seven days. David had an estimated PTA of three *months*.

Once I have the history, I go in for the first time to see the patient. I meet David the second day after he arrives on our unit. A colleague of mine has provided him with a "tilt-in-space" wheelchair. This is a wheelchair that a patient can sit in a neutral position while the entire chair is rotated back. It's like sitting in a rocket cockpit, staring at the ceiling and waiting to lift off. This type of chair is used for a patient who cannot maintain a sitting posture on their own and who often cannot control their head position. He is tilted back and I can see that a percutaneous endoscopic gastronomy (PEG) tube is in place where the nurses will provide him with fluids and nutrients. David is not able to eat or drink anything as food and fluids would just as likely go into his lungs as they would into his stomach. There is a scar at the base of his throat that tells me at one time David had a trach tube inserted so that machines were able to breathe for him. He has a large surgical scar where the surgeons removed and later replaced the large piece of his skull. He has a "foot drop" splint on his right foot that was made to try and maintain his ankle in a functional position when the muscles of his right leg had become spastic, causing his foot to turn down and inwards. His right leg is also stiff, and he cannot keep his foot on the footplate of the chair. His head is rotated to the side and bent forward. He is very stiff and not moving at all. I introduce myself and tell him who I am: "...I'll be one of your therapists while you are here." He says nothing and he has "the stare."

The "stare" after a brain injury is the look of vacancy, a distant stare focusing on a distant unknown spot with little blinking and an unnatural stillness of the eyes. Where most people's eyes are dynamic and constantly searching the environment and the visual details of a subject, a brain injured patient's eyes are unnaturally still and a certain giveaway of a brain injury. It can be unsettling to the casual observer, but I see it often. I use a couple of icebreaker jokes I keep handy and he doesn't laugh. I think to myself, "This is bad, because I know I'm hilarious and he's not responding." He says nothing, moves nothing, and stares right through me. I later write in my notes that the patient is severely dysbulic. The extreme form is abulia. It's the complete lack of the ability to initiate doing anything. It isn't a lack of motivation, laziness, or an unwillingness to move; instead, David's brain has no *ability* to initiate. It's as if his brain is a computer with hardware, software programs, and memory, but no operating system to coordinate and start any process; consequently, he doesn't move or speak. He needs help to do everything. I need to physically move him to get him started. The first time I get him out of his chair, I get a second person to help me and we get him onto our therapy mat. David doesn't help much; in fact, he makes it more difficult as he tries to help, pushing and moving in ways that are uncoordinated, unnatural, and unproductive. When his brain does initiate movement, it tries to cope with the new reality it finds itself in and has a difficult time processing all the senses and coming up with responses in the form of movement that is useful and productive. David cannot stand. He cannot sit by himself. He cannot do anything. I think to myself — and keep it to myself, well hidden from David and his family — that if I can get this man back home, it will be a miracle. He'll

9

probably always need a wheelchair and someone to take care of him. I hope I can get him home.

And so begins the rehab. Every day we work together on his posture, range of motion, strength, and most of all continuous rhythmic motion to try and get David to maintain movement once we get him started. In the beginning, he sustains very little movement. Once we get him going, he gradually slows down and grinds to a halt, stuck, frozen, catatonic, and we "kickstart" him again. We use sports to try and tap into David's natural abilities and into the routines he must have done hundreds of times as an athlete. We use arm bikes with a flywheel to maintain motion. We toss and play with basketballs and soccer balls. Using activities a patient enjoys can be dangerous though. It can be a source of motivation and enjoyment during an extremely difficult time, but it can also be a constant reminder of everything the patient has lost and how difficult everything has become. David, though, responds well to it. He improves to the point that we can have him sit safely in a regular wheelchair. Our goal is to have him sit for one hour each day.

We begin teaching him how to propel the wheelchair on his own. This chair has no foot pedals so that David can use his feet on the floor and "walk" his chair while sitting. He can also use his hands on the push rims of the wheel, but David cannot do any of these things. He cannot coordinate his limbs to move the chair and when he does, he takes a couple of weak strides and grinds to a halt again. Rehab isn't always pretty and it's not always based on fancy book learning either; sometimes it's just getting practical and real. To help David move with his feet in the chair, I sit on a very short rolling stool in front of him, bend down and grab his feet (one hand on each shoe) and walk his feet forward. We walk that way down the halls of the hospital, me moving backwards on my stool and walking David's feet one after another to get a rhythm going, and we do this for hundreds of steps. David's progress is slow at first but it's steady, and everyday he's getting better.

David is also talking more and responding better to conversation. (I know he's getting better because he now smiles and laughs at my jokes. He's obviously a great young man because he thinks I'm hilarious, too — at least that's how I remember it.) In the weeks that follow, David continues to improve. He learns to stand and transfer with supervision from his wheelchair to his bed. He isn't safe though, and often he'll stand and try to start walking. If he does this when no one is around, he could very likely fall and hurt himself again with devastating results. We put a seat belt on the chair that he has trouble undoing himself in order to protect him for the time being. He continues to improve until he is safe enough to walk short distances by himself and get into bed independently. This he does often. Whenever he gets the chance, he gets back into bed. It's not an uncommon behaviour when recovering from a brain injury. It's common enough to have earned its own term: we call it "bed seeking".

David's brain still wants to shut down; it's still is having problems with initiating and continuing through an entire activity. His brain's operating system is working but "crashes" often. He has re-learned how to move, re-learned how to walk, get dressed, eat, brush his teeth, and basically take care of himself, but getting him to do it is another thing.

Left on his own, he is likely to do nothing for hours at a time. Again, it's not lack of motivation, depression, or lack of interest; it's the physiological inability of his brain to start and maintain an activity. He still needs to be prodded and pushed to do almost anything. When he does complete an activity, the quality is often poor. He will brush his teeth adequately, but he may emerge from his room with toothpaste around his mouth, needing a "heads up" to go and have another look in the mirror. With continued support and patience from all the staff and his family, David improves to the point where he can safely even make himself some lunch — but only if he uses the microwave and not the stovetop because he may walk away and take too long to return. This would make the microwave safe enough but not the stove.

There is no doubt that David has come a long way from the time of his admission. It has been almost three months since his admission, but he has recovered better than I had hoped, better than I would have guessed ... and thankfully he has proven me wrong when it comes to my initial doubts about his recovery. He is walking and talking and has ditched the wheelchair entirely. We have beat the odds, but I am not satisfied. I want more for him. He has proven me wrong but has also demonstrated a continued improvement without plateauing. I want to refer him to the Halvard Jonson Center (HJC) in Ponoka, Alberta. The HJC has a brain injury rehabilitation centre that could continue David's rehabilitation for several months more, much longer than what the Glenrose Rehabilitation Hospital's role as a tertiary rehab hospital could provide. Unfortunately, David will not agree to this plan. He has been in one hospital and then another for eight months now and he wants to go home. He wants to continue with his rehabilitation at home on his own and with his family and friends helping him out to keep him active. I have serious reservations about the outcome of this plan. Yes, he has demonstrated improvements beyond our imagination, but he also demonstrates a continued severe lack of initiation. I do not believe that he will be successful in continuing to improve on his own and despite his tremendous recovery, his future at the age of 26 is still very uncertain. But this is not my call. The patient is the boss and my employer, and as such he gets to call the shots. So David and I end our patient-therapist relationship, and David goes home. I should have been satisfied, as we had already accomplished what was unthinkable three months before. I should have been satisfied, but I was not. Thankfully, however, this was not the last I would see of David Raborn.

Immediately as David leaves the hospital, his bed is given to the next patient and my focus has to change to the next case. Weeks pass—maybe months—when one day he appears in the hallway of the Glenrose to start therapy in the outpatient services. We share an enthusiastic hello and are both surprised with how much time has passed. David looks good and appears to be doing well. He is a little more dynamic, but I can still see a lack of initiation in his conversation and he still has the stare. I will continue to run into him in the Glenrose hallways over the next couple of years, and every time I see him, there is a notable improvement in his conversation and the stare lessens until it becomes indistinguishable to me. Whenever I see him, it gives me a smile for the rest of the day. Eventually I hear from David that he was successful in getting his driver's license again, and I'm told he has started working with some assistance at

13

the University of Alberta. The next time I see David, it's on video screens in the Glenrose Hospital showing how he has gotten back on his bicycle again, almost five years after his accident, and he is riding to raise money for the Glenrose Foundation. And then before long, I get the voice message that begins with, "Hi, this is David Raborn; I don't know if you remember me…"

Of course I remember you, David. I remember you every time I see a new patient and feel overwhelmed with their injuries and wonder what I can do for them. I remember you every time a patient's family wonders what kind of future their son, daughter, wife, or husband will have. I remember you every time I hear the medical adage that recovery after a brain injury probably won't go beyond two years. In fact, often when I hear doubts of a good recovery for a patient, I'm the one to say, "Yes, their injuries are bad. But remember David Raborn." Actually, I don't think I could forget David even if I wanted to, especially now that his face is on every television screen in the building. The TVs flip through photos of David and his friends on their bikes for the Glenrose Foundation Charity ride and he looks healthy and happy. Now I see his face every day and I can't escape it…but I don't mind; it still makes me smile.

3. Two Good Samaritans Save the Day
Robbie Lloyd with Bob and Connie Lloyd

It was an unusually nice late summer evening on September 22nd, 2011 when my dad and I were driving along Range Road 223 in Strathcona County near the Richlyn Estates subdivision on our way to Fort Saskatchewan for my hockey tryout. We were in a rush because it was the final tryout for Midget AAA, and the coach wouldn't accept us being late. We had taken my truck, a souped-up red Chevy Extreme.

From about half a mile away, my dad spotted something dark ahead in the middle of the road; we immediately thought a deer or moose had been hit because there was quite a large patch of blood on the road. As we got closer, my dad warned me to look away as I don't deal well with blood. It was then that he realized it was a guy lying there. We parked my truck to block traffic, and my dad approached the guy and asked if he was all right, although we could immediately tell that he wasn't okay; it looked like he'd been a victim of a hit-and-run. Dad told me to avert my eyes and call 9-1-1, which I did.

I stayed near my truck to make sure that no one who was coming over the crest would run over the guy as my dad dealt with dragging him off the road. The guy was lucid, and Dad asked him if someone had hit him. The guy said he'd done this to himself; he'd fallen off his bike. He kept trying to take his helmet off and dad told him to leave it. He also gave Dad his father's name and phone number. Dad phoned the guy's father and told him what we thought had happened as far as we could tell.

As I waited on the side of the road, I counted vehicles that drove by to avoid watching the scene in front of me as I was queasy. No less than 25 cars passed us without stopping to ask if we needed help. A farmer in the field next to where we were was watching as he worked and didn't offer us any assistance either. We got the sense that everyone who passed us assumed that we had hit the guy, and they just weren't going to get involved. Meanwhile, I was trying to stay calm while my dad held the guy in his arms in the ditch and we waited for the paramedics to arrive.

Once the ambulance arrived and the guy's dad got there, the attendants told us we were free to go as there was nothing else we could do. We carried on to hockey and I obviously couldn't focus at all; my dad and I were both pretty messed up. When we got home and told mom about it, all Dad could think about was all the blood; he'd never seen so much blood. The guy's head looked like hamburger meat, he said. He also said the guy looked kind of grubby and rough so he was concerned about the amount of blood all over himself which he really hadn't thought of at the time as he had been functioning on auto-pilot.

Mom told Dad to follow up with Dr. Raborn the next day, since we had his phone number. As his son was coherent and chatty when we left him, we were positive he probably had some nasty bruises, scrapes, and maybe a concussion. But when Dad talked to Dr. Raborn the next day, his son, David, had already undergone two surgeries and his prognosis was not good. We were shocked.

We have kept in close touch thereafter, visited David in the hospital a few times, and continue to keep up with his progress. We felt very connected to the Raborn family from that moment, and we still do to this day.

4. NOT ADMITTED
Diane Raborn

Reaching into my soul to gather thoughts to share with others regarding the events of the afternoon of the 22nd of September 2011 is not easy.

I thought I'd be able to handle it well by this time. Writing is second nature to me. Therefore, it's inexplicable to me to find my heart in such a scattered place. I will do my best to piece things together with words that will do justice to David's worthy project. It is meaningful to share and is something that needs to be shared.

In an attempt to express my thoughts, my mind explodes with vivid pictures captured from a timeless place washing over me with immediate horror. Behind me is a woman from the clergy who suddenly appears almost out of nowhere. She is physically holding me up in a curtain-drawn area as a medical team suddenly surrounds Dave. They are desperately trying to save his life, having been brought in by 'code-blue.'

The sounds and sights are brutally harsh. The pictures hidden in the pocket recesses of my brain cause me, even now, to breathe fast and shallow as I remember the shouts and smells of the moment when it becomes clear in the Grey Nuns Hospital that no one anticipated what is currently happening. The chaplain is now praying with me as Dave has gone from being seemingly coherent, though in pain, to being in severe and dire distress.

The moments following are a blur. The same ambulance that took him from the rural road where the accident happened to the Grey Nuns is now transporting him to the University of Alberta Hospital for surgery. I remember the white faces of the medical staff. We, Dave's dad (Wayne) and I, are not allowed to come. I'd called David's brother, Taylor, who was finishing his PhD at the University of Iowa, and I still remember the surreal feeling as we spoke. To this day, it is the hardest thing I've ever had to do. "Pray," I say. *"Just pray."*

Lorne and Rita Penner were with us, as were Janet Mador and her daughter, Lauren, Dave's friend. Janet and Lauren had been having dinner together and received the call while in a restaurant. They came immediately. Janet mentions later that when she arrived at the Grey Nuns Hospital, the chaplain was with me in full "prayer mode". Dave is being intubated in an area of organized chaos around the examining table where Dave is fighting, losing control, and slipping away. Wayne is there with the medical team and is very calming. To calm myself, Janet shares that I disappear outside for a couple of minutes several times throughout this ordeal. Although I have no remembrance of 'leaving the scene', so to speak, I'm sure it was a desperate move to clear my head enabling me to keep myself from falling apart.

Lorne and Rita drove us, with Janet and Lauren following, to the University of Alberta Hospital. I do recall Wayne and I sitting stunned, holding each other close. The next thing that comes to mind is trying to find David in this large metropolitan hospital located in the heart of the University of Alberta. Janet and Rita are with me, and we are racing around searching for him. He's not listed in emergency

18

and his name isn't known at any desk we check. This has us all frantic, trying to figure out where David is located. Throughout this blur of a time, I have pictures of Rita, Janet and me running in hospital halls. *Searching. Running and searching.*

However, the reason he wasn't admitted to the U of A Hospital is quite valid: David was taken immediately to the operating room, where Dr. Michael Chow and his amazing team are prepping for surgery with the clock ticking. We're later told that he was "cutting skin" within fifteen minutes of David's arrival. This was one of four or five emergency neurosurgical operations that David would incur at his stay at the U of A. Obviously, we are beyond thankful for what Dr. Michael Chow and his team did numerous times for us, for David.

In the hospital, there were *many* angels who consistently and constantly helped; however, there was one in the form of a friend who stands out. Janet Mador came almost every day. She helped me in so many ways. Her presence was a major contributing factor in lifting our family's spirit. As a nurse, her knowledge was invaluable. As a former ICU nurse, she was crucial in helping with the day-to-day routine.

As a fifteen-year old, I decided to be a candy striper at our university's public hospital. Should I be involved in medicine, business, or education? What was my calling? My friend, Susan Meyer (Sinyai), and I volunteered weekly, walking from our local high school to UNC Memorial Hospital.

It was, indeed, an eye-opener. It didn't take long to learn that hospitals and I did not belong together. The very smell of blood, the very sight of medical uniforms, and the very act of stepping through the hospital doors caused my body to dissolve. I fainted twice in three days! "*She's hit the floor again.*" Having been in this same hospital off and on for a year at the age of four with glomerulonephritis, my hospital sensibilities were low. My answer: "*Stay away from hospitals.*"

I did a very good job of avoiding hospitals for a long time.

Thankfully, my friend Janet came to the hospital following Dave's accident bringing friendship, practical support, and much-welcomed hot morning coffee. When we were called into a conference room with the hospital staff, often receiving devastating news, Janet agreed to come with us, lending phenomenal support.

Janet worked years earlier in the ICU of the University of Alberta Hospital when it occupied the old brick building. She helped with 'range of motion' techniques that I'd been given to apply and with everything else "medical"—the things that made me melt just by the fact that they were in the hospital. Her nursing skills shone through with much-needed competency and calmness. And they were certainly beneficial to us all during this long, protracted journey in the Neuro ICU and neurological ward with our son. My friend Janet walked me through it and, more importantly, walked with me. It was this wonderful friend with whom I knew I could be myself during the harsh reality that was our son's severe traumatic brain injury. And, remarkably, at times we even laughed. Such as when Rita spotted the hair dye kit that Wayne placed in my oversize purse. Rita, Janet and I found a washroom tucked away in an obscure place; and, *voila*, I was soon ready to meet my family arriving from out of province.

I will always be extraordinarily grateful.

5. WILL HE EVER SPEAK AGAIN?
Dr. Caroline Musselwhite, with email from Mary Caldwell

I think the way that Mary expressed this is so powerful: *"David is the only one with his brain and with this injury—you can only compare him to him."*

And about the program, my suggestion to Diane when Mary sent this was: "Divide and conquer"—get all of David's friends to pitch in.

First, share the "Approach the patient" with EVERYONE!! I believe his mom actually made a poster about this.

Second, I suggested that she put one of David's friends in charge of each area (visual stimulation, auditory stimulation, etc.), and then they could assemble the needed materials, and share this with other friends.

My memory is that David went from a 4 to a 7 on the Glasgow Scale within 48 or 72 hours of initiating this program. Obviously, that could have been coincidence, but given that he had made minimal progress the few days before this program was initiated, I feel that it had a positive impact. It also gave a clear way for his friends and family to feel like they were participating in his recovery, not just sitting and hoping!!!

From: Mary Caldwell
Subject: David's progress
Date: October 4, 2011 at 5:02:22 PM MST
To: Caroline Musselwhite

Hey Diane, I am Mary Caldwell, a friend of Carolyn's. I learned about your son's accident through her. I am a speech pathologist who specialized in closed head injury while I was at Duke. I have a few suggestions that may help. Carolyn said that David is 13 days out. Please know that in the world of head injury that is one minute. I am not writing to give false hope, just hope. The biggest thing to remember is that no one knows what David's course will be. David is the only one with his brain and with this injury. You can only compare him to him. His age and extreme health with so many sports promoting ambidextrous ability are all very good signs for him. The fact that he already knows how to push himself is terrific for him. If you can have a head injury on a better side, he did. The right has far fewer long-term problems than does the left. Generally speaking, the right is visually based, math, patterns, melody, and the left is language, logic, and reasoning.

Carolyn said that David is Glasgow level 4. There are 11 more to go. I attached a copy of coma stimulation. The brain works by afferent and efferent neurons. If you touch David on the foot and he moves his arm or head, that is an undifferentiated response: you put information in and you got information back. You evoked, or elicited, brain activity. If

22

he gets a needle in his arm and grimaces and moves his arm away, that is a differentiated response—a much higher level on the coma scale. The 12 cranial nerves activate all four lobes of the brain on the left and right side. The five senses activate all 12 cranial nerves. So, using the five senses you can activate brain activity throughout the brain. You don't have to wait for his recovery; you can start now. Use opposite input, light touch, deep pressure, music he likes and music he would never listen to, smells that are considered good and bad, things that are cool and hot, rough and smooth. Carolyn can tell you about single switches to start communication and improve responses. I have attached some techniques for coma stimulation below if you want to start there. Good luck, and stay strong. This is the long haul.

Techniques of Coma Stimulation
Approaching the patient
- Identify yourself.
- Talk to the patient slowly and in a normal tone of voice.
- Keep sentences short and give the patient extra time to think about what you've said.
- Orient patient to the date, time, place, and reason for being in the hospital, and explain to the patient what you are going to do.

Visual Stimulation
- Provide a visually stimulating environment at the bedside, such as colourful, familiar objects, family photographs (labeled), and TV for 10-15 minutes at a time.

- Provide normal visual orientation, by positioning patient upright in bed, in the wheelchair, etc. This also helps decrease complications of prolonged bedrest, such as pressure sores, breathing problems, osteoporosis, and muscle contractures.

- Eliminate distraction to allow patient to focus on visual stimuli, such as a familiar face, object, photos, and a mirror.

- Attempt visual tracking after focusing is established (i.e., getting the patient to follow a stimulus with his/her eyes at it moves). Tracking usually begins in the centre or midline.

Auditory Stimulation
- Provide regular auditory stimulation at the patient's bedside. All hospital staff should be encouraged to speak to the patient as they work in the room or directly with the patient. An information sheet can be posted in the room with information about the patient's likes and dislikes.

- Permit only one person to speak at a time.

- Use radio, TV, a tape recording of a familiar voice, etc., for 10-15 minutes at intervals throughout the day. Direct work to focusing and localizing sound, and look for patient's response when you change the location of a sound (e.g., call the patient's name, clap your hands, ring a bell, shake a rattle, blow a whistle, etc., for 5-10 seconds at a time).

- Avoid stimulation that evokes a startled response. This type of stimulation is counterproductive.

Touch Stimulation

- Tactile input can be facilitory (encourage a desired response) or inhibitory (discourage/interfere with a desired response). For example, pain and light touch to the skin tend to produce an inhibitory response, while maintained touch, pressure to the oral area, and slow stroking of the spine tend to produce a facilitory response. The face, and especially the lips and mouth area, are the most sensitive.
- Use a variety of textures, such as personal clothing, blankets, stuffed animals, lotions, etc.
- Use a variety of temperatures, such as warm and cold cloths or metal spoons dipped for 30 seconds in hot or cold water.
- Vary the degree of pressure: firm pressure is usually less threatening or irritating to the patient than light touch. Examples include grasping a muscle and maintaining the pressure for 3-5 seconds, stretching a tendon and maintaining the stretch for a few seconds, or rubbing the sternum.
- Use unpleasant stimuli, such as a pinprick, with caution. Avoid ice to face or body as it may trigger a sympathetic nervous system response (i.e., increased blood pressure, heart rate and salivation, and decreased gastrointestinal activity).

Movement Stimulation

- Use range of motion exercises, changes in body position such as a single or repetitive roll, a tilt table to bring the patient to a more upright position, and movement activities on a therapy mat.
- Watch for early physical protective reactions or

delayed balance reactions during these activities.

Position Stimulation
- Slow changes in position tend to be inhibitory, while faster movement patterns tend to facilitate arousal.
- Monitor the patient's blood pressure (and ICP if appropriate) during this stimulation.
- Use position changes that are meaningful and familiar, such as rolling, rocking in a chair or on a mat, and moving from laying down to sitting.
- Avoid spinning, which may trigger seizures, and mechanical input, such as raising and lowering the hospital bed, which has little functional meaning and produces limited response.

Smell Stimulation
- Use aftershave, cologne, perfume, flavoured extracts, coffee grounds, shampoo, and favourite foods.
- Provide the stimuli for no more than 10 seconds.
- Avoid touching the skin with the scent because the patient may accommodate the scent and be less responsive to it.
- Use garlic and mustard as noxious stimuli.
- Avoid vinegar and ammonia because they irritate the trigeminal nerve.

However, there may not be a response to smell stimulation because:
- The olfactory nerve is the most commonly injured cranial nerve in TBI;
- Many TBI patients have tracheostomies, which eliminate the exchange of air through the nostrils

and therefore inhibit the sense of smell;

- Patients have nasogastric tubes in place, which
  block one nostril and, therefore, decrease the sense
  of smell.

Taste and Oral Stimulation

- Provide taste stimulation, unless patient is prone to
  aspiration: use a cotton swab dipped in a sweet,
  salty, or sour solution, but avoid sweet tastes if the
  patient has difficulty managing oral secretions since
  sweet tastes increase salivation.
- Provide oral stimulation during routine mouth care,
  unless patient
  demonstrates a bite reflex.
- Use a sponge-tipped or glycerin swab or a soft
  toothbrush to diminish hypersensitivity and
  abnormal oral/facial reflexes.
- Use a flavoured cleansing agent, such as mint or
  lemon, to increase oral stimulation during routine
  mouth care.
- Provide stimulation to the lips and the area around
  the mouth. If patient demonstrates defensiveness to
  touch, such as pursing lips, closing mouth, or pulling
  away from the stimulus, gently continue with
  stimulation techniques to decrease defensive
  reactions and increase level of awareness. Do not
  attempt to feed patients in coma.

Diane made a copy of the above advice and encouraged
(*nagged*) the doctors to keep it in the main file and refer to it,
and they showed her that they did. She thinks the results
must have changed many of the doctors' minds.

6. AN MD FOR AN AUNT
Dr. Cindy Shumpert

I remember being at the hospital the first week David was there. It was in September; he was unconscious, in the ICU, with massive brain swelling and with one pupil fixed and dilated. From a medical standpoint, the pupil was the biggest worry to me. That usually means the base of the brain (which controls basic functions like breathing) has herniated down out of the skull. It is basically **not reversible**. I am not sure what the CAT scans showed at that point. All I know is that I prayed for one thing only: if his injuries were not reversible, for God to take David home with Him, and if they **were** reversible, to return him to us **whole**. That was about four or five days after his injury.

I had been sleeping on my trusty backpacking sleep pad with my summer sleeping bag in the corner of the ICU. This is apparently illegal. So at around 3:00 in the morning, bright flashlights suddenly shone in my face, with the security police demanding to know who I am and why I am there. In order to be permitted to stay (in the waiting room, though, not in the ICU), I had to give them David's name and room number (which they did verify). The next morning, when we went in to see David, the nurse told us, "Both of his pupils are reactive!" I commented, "That is not possible," and he said, "Well, they are reactive this morning!" Then he showed us this TOTAL MIRACLE!!

Fast forward to November; David was out on the main floor. I flew up from the Atlanta area for another week, and immediately saw that David was conscious ... well, sort of. His mom said to him, "Aunt Cindy is here. What do you think of that?" David had a whiteboard to write on, and after a short hesitation, David wrote: "I'm so excited!" This was all written *by David* exactly like that, with the capital letter, apostrophe, and exclamation point all correct. I turned to Diane (David's mom) and said, "He's going to be fine!" I knew his brain was intact inside that skull!

Diane and I would stand at the end of the bed and sing: *"Oh, do your ears hang low? Do they wobble to and fro..."* and promise to quit singing it if David would talk to us. (David was nonverbal at that point). I was told the day after I left to go home that David started talking. I guess he knew he was safe from ever hearing that song from us again!
 (It was so cold and snowy in Edmonton that November that I had to buy a pair of fur-lined boots in the lobby of the hospital, just to walk back and forth to the parking lot. Now I know why I live in Georgia.)

One of the issues I faced occurred in November at the U of A Hospital, when David was on the main floor, not in the ICU. The nurse came in and turned off his feeding tube. When we asked why, we were told he was having surgery in the morning. We had been given no notice of any surgery! I went out and talked to the nurse, who was quite rude to me. She told me that:

1. It was to replace the bone on David's skull.
2. They did **not** have to tell us or get permission from anybody to take David to surgery.
3. There was no one available to talk to us about the procedure, as it was very late.

So I said we would **not** tolerate that, and that **no** surgery would be done until someone talked to us. About three hours later, the senior resident did come speak with us. He was nice but apparently didn't understand that it should be illegal for a surgeon to operate on anyone without permission from patient or next of kin (except in an emergency, of course, which this was decidedly **not**). I guess Canadian rules are different from American rules. You can get sued for doing surgery in the U.S. without permission. However, we'd also be in debt for a million years after being in the hospital for eight months, had this happened in the U.S.!

Fast forward to late February, when David got into rehab. I came for another visit. The first day I was there, David finally had a swallowing test done. I had requested it at the hospital in November, but I guess socialized medicine does have its drawbacks. David passed the second time taking the test. So for lunch the next day, he had his first solid food since September. He wolfed it down, and I thought he might grab his tablemate's too, if he thought he would have gotten away with it. I remember that lunch like it was yesterday. "I hadn't eaten solid food in almost half a year, and they gave me tater tots with lots of ketchup! I was one happy man!" David told me later. So that afternoon, I went with David to physical therapy. He walked for the first time—about 50 metres, I think. I walked behind with the wheelchair. When we were done, I was wheeling him back to the unit, and I asked, "Aren't you excited that you walked today?" David's reply was: *"I'm excited about supper!"*

7. WONDERFUL NEIGHBOURS
Pastor Rita Penner

It had been over 24 hours since my phone had rung and I heard the trembling voice of Diane, my dear friend and neighbour: "David's been in a bad bike accident. We're on our way to the ER." My heart plummeted as I responded, "We're coming." Now the next evening, my husband and I, together with about 35 others were in the waiting area outside of ICU at the U of A hospital.

Word of the accident had spread quickly and because David and his family were dearly loved by many, the group just continued to grow. The prospect for David was very grim. The medical community had done everything they possibly could but it didn't seem like it would be enough. Out in that waiting area we did what people in similar circumstances have done for thousands of years: we made a large circle and holding hands, we prayed. We prayed passionately that God would intervene on David's behalf and do for him what no one else could—turn the tide and begin a healing process that would lead to life!

Together we declared, "God, we need a miracle." God in His kindness did intervene, and in mercy began David on a journey of recovery. David's life was spared, and his family, friends, and many others who would hear his story later and be touched by His beautiful life, were given a miracle for which we are all eternally grateful!

8. "A FORTUNATE FELLOW"
Lorne Penner, LLB

I will always remember the night of September 22nd, 2011 as I was on my way home from the airport. My wife called me and told me that David had been hurt. He had been in a bicycle accident and had been picked up by the ambulance and was on his way to the Grey Nuns Hospital.

My wife Rita and I immediately went to the hospital to be with the family. Our good friends Janet Mador and her daughter Lauren were already there assisting the family. Shortly thereafter, it was determined that he should be moved the University of Alberta Hospital for potential surgery. This was to be the beginning of a very long and arduous time for David and his family.

Sometime during that night or the next day (the time runs together a bit), the neurosurgeon met with David's parents, with us present as their support. The doctor gave a grim prognosis with the immediate decision being whether or not to intubate. Wayne and Diane said "yes" without hesitation, and they never wavered from their strong belief that David would one day recover from this dreadful event.

My wife and I, along with David, Janet and Lauren Mador, spent many evenings at the hospital trying our best to support the family while David was in a coma. During this time, Lauren and many, many, many of David's friends showed up regularly, and as I recall, we even had a large Thanksgiving dinner for 30 or more people at the hospital, arranged by Leah and Dylan Karch with the help of friends.

Taylor (David's brother) and a number of cousins and aunts of Diane's (David's mother) often flew in from the U.S. to visit, and Frances Fletcher (David's grandmother) manned the telephones at home, with at least two phones at a time carried in her apron.

On two occasions, David had to have half of his skullcap removed to help relieve the pressure on his brain. He also had to battle a couple of rounds of C. difficile, a nasty gastrointestinal bug. Looking on from the outside, it was hard to see how he would survive the ordeal, and if he did survive, how he would he ever really recover. But he started to turn the corner and begin to heal. His level of consciousness kept getting better and better until he finally went to the Glenrose Hospital to start his rehabilitation.

After arriving at the Glenrose, he steadily improved at what seemed a pretty rapid rate. He had not eaten solid food for many months, and I very much remember the night when there were some tater tots on the table where he was sitting. His father and I were sitting with David, and we were quite concerned that the tots would be a choking hazard for him. However, with great determination, David impressed upon us that he wanted those tots. I have never seen anyone enjoy any food as much as David enjoyed those fries that night. David's rehab continued until he was soon walking on his own. He returned home and continued with rehab at the Glenrose as an outpatient.

David was a very fortunate fellow to have had such wonderful care from the University and Glenrose hospitals, but the real heroes of the story are his parents. Long after most people would have given up all hope, they persisted in confidence that he would recover. Day after day after day, I would encounter Wayne and David diligently walking around the subdivision where we live, building David's strength and coordination. I have truly been amazed at David's recovery and the wonders of healing that have occurred in his brain. I consider myself fortunate to have witnessed this great feat of endurance and recovery.

9. "I BELIEVE IN YOU"
Dr. Christine Botchway

Truly, I recall it as though it were yesterday. So deeply on my soul are the events and thoughts etched and so vivid the memories, that I know their colour, light, and brilliance will not diminish or ever fail to humble and draw into awe my very being on the subject of faith, prayer, and healing.

Indeed these events that I was so privileged to witness, in contemplation of or in relating this awe-inspiring testimony as I often do, reflect the majestic glory of our God and the power He releases when we speak according to His words and activate here on earth His holy will in vibrant prayers of faith.

It was an ordinary day. I was at home doing ordinary chores and all was quite ordinary ... except that I had an uncharacteristic urging to check my Facebook page. Finding nothing much on my business or personal pages, I was about to sign out when for some reason I clicked on Diane Raborn's Facebook page. At first glance I noticed there were quite a few comments on what I originally thought was a prayer discussion. Not being one who normally delights in reading Facebook comments, I again was about to sign out when my eye caught one comment and then another. It seemed to me that this was no general prayer discussion but was focused on someone specific.

I wondered for whom they were praying. I continued to read the comments and posts. Then a name came up — I think it was in one of Diane's posts. The person who was the subject of this intense Facebook discussion and prayer was mentioned. They were praying for someone named David.

I remember thinking that sounded vaguely familiar, but I could not quite make the connection, which was locked in the recesses of my mind, so I continued reading to find out why prayer was being offered for this person and who he was. Then someone mentioned another name: Taylor. And the vague recognition began to intensify and then fade like a dream where the gates of the subconscious refuse to release memory into the conscious. Then someone mentioned "David and Taylor."

And that was when the gates of my subconscious mind flung open.

Suddenly I saw in my mind's eye the framed picture of two young boys neatly displayed on the bookshelf of the Dean of the Dental School, Dr. Raborn. Taylor and David were the young boys, perhaps in their mid-teens, in the photos that I looked at every time I snuck into Dr. Raborn's office to borrow or return a book off his bookshelf. They were Dr. Raborn's sons.

Although I had never met them during my five-year academic career at the University of Alberta, I had heard much about them.

I raced through the comments and posts to find out what had happened to David. I could come to no conclusion. But I could tell just by the tone of the conversations that it was very serious. I messaged Diane and asked her what had happened.

I can't quite remember if I called Diane or she called me, but we connected that same day. Diane communicated that her son David had been riding his bike, as he loved to do, when he had crashed and sustained a serious head injury. He had been wearing his bike helmet and had been following all safety rules. He had been rushed to the University of Alberta Hospital and surgery had been performed to save his life.

I told Diane I would be praying along with all the other people who were sending in prayers and encouragement and support in prayer. Diane said he was receiving visitors and invited us to come by the hospital.

After hanging up the phone, I prayed for David, Diane, and Dr. Raborn. I could almost tangibly feel the pain of this dark gloomy time. I prayed for peace and healing. Then I called John, my husband, and told him what had happened. He was very sorry to hear it. I told him to clear his schedule because we were going to visit the Raborns.

It was a gloomy, cold night when John and I arrived at the University of Alberta Hospital. I remember making our way up to the ward where David was. When we entered the room, I noticed it was a double-occupied room. David was in the inner area of the room, and the curtain was partially drawn. Dr. Raborn greeted us first as we came in, and as we progressed into the room we saw Diane. She greeted us with great enthusiasm, which I had often noticed she possessed. Diane has always exhibited great measures of joy and optimism. I had always found chatting with her a delightful experience simply because she was so interesting and so full of rare grace and nobility.

I had been tense coming into the ward, considering how devastating it must be for parents to see their beloved child injured; the more I thought about it, the more I could feel that pain. I had wondered how Diane would be holding up. I had worked with Dr. Raborn for five years and was fairly sure that on the outside he would be strong and calm, and he surely was.

Diane thanked us for coming and enthusiastically told us what great progress David was making. She took us right up to his bed.

David was sitting up in bed. He was pale and his eyes did not quite make contact with us, or at least not for long. There was no expression on his face at all. The most shocking and obvious thing was a huge dent in his skull. I remember feeling physical pain shoot down my entire body as I thought of how much pain he must have endured as he crashed on his head.

I had worked in my early days as a dentist with patients with such skull injuries, including with a man who had suffered a similar injury and whose skull had never been repaired. While all these thoughts were racing through my mind, I heard Diane introduce me to David. She said, "David, this is Dr. Christine Botchway and her husband, John..."

David gave no indication that he had heard or understood. Diane continued to speak to him, going into detail about both John and me.

David did not respond.

Diane picked up a writing board and propped it up on David's lap, and then she placed a pen marker in his hand. I watched as he struggled to even hold the pen. His fingers appeared stiff and almost paralyzed, but there was just a hint of movement. Diane stuck the pen back between his fingers each time it slipped. "He has been writing today," she said cheerfully.

The pen slipped from David's grip. "Oh," said Diane repositioning it again. "I think he wants to write something."

David's fingers grasped around the pen, shaking as he tried to hold the pad close to the pen.

John began to talk about something else, and we temporarily took our focus off David's struggle to hold the pen.

Diane showed me some get well cards and notes that had been sent to David. That was when I noticed the way the hospital room had been set up: Diane had almost transformed it into a regular, albeit tiny, bedroom. On the walls were pictures, inspirational notes, and messages. Familiar, favourite, and inspirational things were all around David. Diane explained that this was really important, to show him that his friends and former teammates were there with him, thinking and praying for him. Now and again she would pull out an interesting card and take it to David to show him.

I did not see David respond or indicate he could hear or understand us, but Diane never once faltered. She spoke to him as though she knew and saw something we could not. She did not speak to him as though she hoped he could hear and understand. She spoke to him directly with an authority that declared: "You can hear me. You can understand. You are healed."

John had moved away slightly and was talking to Dr. Raborn. But I was watching and listening carefully to Diane. I could feel the tangible energy of faith—genuine faith—rising up in that small hospital room. I could feel the sound of Diane's voice speaking faith continually and unceasingly, and amidst the calm peace something I could not see but could feel was manifesting. Diane had taken all the expressions of faith and love and goodwill, and along with Dr. Raborn and Taylor, had built a fortress of faith around David. Wherever my eyes looked, there were words from which healing burst forth. There were pictures from which joy escaped, and as David lay expressionless on his bed, I could almost see faith dancing all around him.

Diane told me that she had been playing a CD of mine for David. One of the songs was a song I wrote for my daughter Vienna when she was two. It was called *"I Believe in You."* It was a really simple song from the heart about a mother's pure unfailing love for her child.

I had been contemplating how best to plant in the heart of my daughter the knowledge that knowing who she was in God would forever enable her to overcome any adversity of the world and any arrow of the enemy. I had been looking at her years prior as she innocently played with her fluffy ponytails, recognizing that I was charged with the awesome task of helping her to learn about her awesome powerful identity in Yeshua when this song flowed into my mind.

We prayed for David. There had been many prayers in that room and around that bed. We added our words charged with faith and love and belief in our God who heals. Then Diane asked me to sing a song. I think I sang "Amazing Grace" quietly. Diane kept praising God. Nothing but positive, uplifting, good things came out of her mouth. She seemed at perfect peace.

Somewhere in between singing, praying, and standing in that fortress of faith where I could feel the energy was different from that outside of it, where the peace within it was different from the hustle and bustle outside of it, where words of faith were activating the will of God, some minute portion of my soul began to resonate in understanding.

I looked at David, and then I looked at Diane, and then at the wall and the words by which Dr. Raborn was standing, chatting with John. Understanding came to me. She was calling things that are not as things that are in direct obedience to God's word.

This was warfare in action.

I thought to myself that it is easy not to see the power of the warriors of God until the darkness of the battle arises and then all that light within them slays the darkness of doubt.

We had been there a while and John said it was time to go. We bid the Raborns a good night and said goodbye to David, blessing him with all of God's blessings.

But Diane stopped us. "Wait," she said. "David wants to say something to you." There was silence. No one said anything.

We all stared at Diane.

Gently she took away the clipboard that had been in David's hands the entire time we had been there. The pen was still clutched in his stiff hand. She handed it to me.

I know my eyes grew round as I stared at the shaky scrawled words painstakingly written over an hour. I stared at the words and then at David and then again at the words. He looked exhausted, as though penning those two words had taken all his strength.

I was humbled for I knew instantaneously that the strength that he possessed to write out those words came from a source whose gates had been ripped open by the onslaught of

41

faith, prayer, praise, and the ceaseless declarations of the warriors of prayer who carried the light of God. I knew that what we had witnessed that night was a practical application of "Thy kingdom come, Thy will be done on earth as in heaven." I handed John the clipboard that said simply:

"Thank you."

I began to praise Our King.

10. BEARDS FOR BROBORN
Kevin Meleskie and Stef Williams

Kevin Meleskie

I remember with stunning clarity the night I found out about Dave's injury. Even though it has been five years, I can recall with frightening ease the phone call I received from our mutual friend, Brennan Lafleur. I remember it being fairly late at night, although Dave had been living this ordeal for quite a few hours prior to my awareness. The phone call went something like this:

Brennan: Hey Kev, uhhh, I'm not too sure of the details, but it sounds like Dave had a pretty bad bike accident and hit his head. He's going into surgery for it.

Me: Oh wow, umm, is it bad? Like he'll be okay, right?

I recall my disbelief at this point. Things like this don't happen to people like David Raborn. He was the life of the party, the fun guy you always want around, and the guy who was good at everything. Bad things don't happen to good people when they are 25 years old; they just don't, I told myself.

Brennan: Oh ya, I think he'll be fine; he'll get through it. Taylor sounded like it was serious, but ya I mean, he'll be okay, right?

What I should tell you at this point is that Brennan is one of the most optimistic people I've ever met; the type of guy to shank a drive (in golf) into the bushes and feel, with complete conviction, that he will find his ball, no problem. When I got off the phone, I was left with an uneasy feeling. Surgery? Like, brain surgery? Surely that is a very big deal. I then chatted with our other friend Nick Dehod about the situation. Nick, though optimistic, had a sense of realism closer to my own. After a few exchanges, Nick and I decided that sleep would likely elude us both, and we decided to head to a late night coffee shop. I took a picture that night that I will hopefully never lose: two guys talking in disbelief over a couple of cups of coffee. I can't speak for Nick, but I know that at that moment, the idea of Dave not making it through that night was only a small fear; it was never a reality. It wasn't until the next day that everything changed.

I can't recall the moment it happened, but at some point the next day, it became clear that this wasn't a fairly routine hospital stay. Up until now, I had thought that Dave may have a week or so in the hospital recovering from his surgery, and I'd visit him to make sure he wasn't scared. I remember being called by someone—the fact I can't remember who still surprises me—and being told, "You need to come to the hospital right now; it's more serious than we thought." I left work, telling my boss that a friend had been in an accident and I needed to see him, and I drove straight to the U of A Hospital. I should mention at this point that I suffer from terrible anxiety over hospitals. The only time I had visited one in the last ten years sent me into a full panic attack, and that was when I visited my dad after a routine surgery for a ruptured Achilles tendon. Until this ordeal, I had an image of hospitals as a negative place, where sick people go and never leave. This experience changed my perspective and rid me of my fears ... but I digress.

After getting into my car and calling my fiancée (who is now my wife), telling her that I would update her as soon as I got there, I sped south to the U of A Hospital—a place I had passed almost every day for four years during my undergraduate degree, all the while still afraid of what lay inside. I found parking and made my way to Neuro ICU, as instructed. "*ICU*" I thought to myself. "*That's really serious, right?*" I made it to the waiting room and joined a small group of friends, which would soon turn into about 15 of us. Dave's closest and oldest friends. As I said my hellos, both to Dave's parents and to the group that had gathered, a bed with a patient rolled by, surrounded by what seemed like ten doctors and nurses. I didn't recognize the person in that bed, but it was my pal Dave. His parents rushed after the bed, and they disappeared into the ICU wing just around the corner from the waiting room in which we were gathered. I don't know about the rest of the group, but it was at that moment that my brain switched from "Yeah, this is serious, but he'll of course be okay; it's just something to push through..." to "Wait; he's going to make it, right?"

44

Some time passed, and the group experienced quite a bit of confusion over the state of Dave's well-being. The optimists reassured everyone that surely everything would be great. After all, our group of ten to fifteen 24-25 year old men and women had barely ever set foot in a hospital, let alone the Neuro ICU wing of the U of A Hospital. The reality of life was about to smack all of us directly in the face. We're not immortal, bad things happen to good people, and people our age die.

One of our good friends Adam, a nurse at the U of A, was called into the mysterious doors that I was petrified to even look through. Through those doors lay patients fighting for their lives. It was a reality I had feared and willfully ignored for my entire life. Some time passed, and I recall Adam and Dave's father, Dr. Raborn, emerging from the door that separated my sense of normalcy from reality. The memory of what happened in the next few minutes will never leave me. Quiet fell over the group of normally rambunctious young men; we gathered in a circle around Dr. Raborn sitting solemnly in a leather chair surrounded by 10 to 15 kids who were the same age as his son who was lying unconscious in a bed 20 metres to his left. To this day, I don't know how he spoke these words with such poise. My memory of what Dr. Raborn said to us is as follows:

"Dave is in a lot of trouble, guys, and he needs your help. They are going to let you in to see him, and Dave needs your positivity and your prayers right now. They are saying he may not make it through the night, so when you see him, please pray for him and send him your love. He needs you."

I am not positive those were his words, but that is what I heard. I suddenly realized that before this moment, none of this had really sunk in at all. I was feeling things, saying things, and going through the appropriate motions, but it didn't feel real.

It suddenly felt very real.

I remember turning and walking away, and Brennan coming to hug me. I felt guilty that I hadn't taken this situation as seriously at first as I should have, that I hadn't realized the gravity of the situation.

As we filed in to see Dave lying in that bed, being kept alive by the miracles of modern medicine, I lost all fear of hospitals; I would have never left if it had meant anything. I was but a small part in Dave's journey, but over the next few months, he taught me the meaning of resilience, of resolution, and of the power of the human body to heal itself. Dave hardly remembers his stay at the U of A Hospital, but his spirit was there 100% of the time, and I'll never forget its power.

Stef Williams

I remember learning about Dave's accident through the wonderful world of social media. Julian's post caught my attention: "David had an accident while riding his bike and is laid up in the hospital. Please post on his wall to show him how much support he has from all the people who love him." My older brother, Mike, was a good friend of Dave's, and I generally got news through him. I hadn't talked to Mike for a couple of days, so I sent him a text message right away asking what was going on.

"He was in a bike accident the other day. It doesn't sound good."

I could tell by the short tone of his text that it was legitimately not good, and the nurse in me wanted to help right away. I had never felt so helpless before in my life; however, I knew that Dave was receiving the best care possible and all we could do was send him prayers and positive vibes to give him the strength to pull through.

For the next week I checked in with my brother on a daily basis for any updates on Dave's condition. As Kevin mentioned, the reality of life began to hit a lot of us hard. We are not immortal, and terrible things can happen to the best of people. I can speak as an outsider who watched Dave's family and friends come together over the next few days, weeks, and months in such a way that words simply cannot describe. His support network came together like a flash mob. I knew Dave was a popular son, brother, athlete, and friend (among many other designations), but I had never seen anything like this. From Day One (when Kevin speaks of 10-15 people gathering together in the waiting room when Dave was rushed to the ICU) through the time that followed, everybody—including his friends and family members in other cities, states, and countries overseas—was reaching out to him and imploring him to use his strength to pull through.

After a few days of rollercoaster emotions and news, his dearest friends (otherwise known as "*bros*") began to snap selfies of themselves growing out patchy beards and moustaches—or whatever fuzz they could grow—in honour and support of their friend Dave. It was my understanding that Dave was a big fan of classy facial hair (beards and moustaches) and had a clean beard of his own. Due to the surgeries, breathing tubes etc., Dave would be growing this beard out for an indeterminate amount of time, and his bros wanted to join in on this (and also get a head start on Movember at the same time, of course). This new trend quickly became known as *"Beards for Broborn."*

Kevin Meleskie

At the end of September, Stef wanted to do more for Dave. Stef couldn't grow a beard, but she had a deep love for arts and crafts and wanted to design something for Dave. She spoke to John Schmidt about the idea of making some T-shirts for the guys to wear so they could explain their beards, and he was sold. He ran the idea by their group of friends, and he came back with one specified request: they need to be the deepest V-neck shirts possible. That's when Stef was prepared to push up her sleeves and design some shirts. She originally planned on making five or six shirts from plain white T-shirts and some iron on letters, but when John got back to her with a (small?) request of nearly 20 shirts, Stef with my help turned to her friends in Toronto. It just so happened that the guys from Spin Ink, who had embarked on a band merchandise company in Toronto, knew Dave from high school in Sherwood Park. When Spin Ink heard about Dave's accident, they immediately offered their services and designed a "*Beards for Broborn*" T-shirt and another that said "*Babes for Broborn,*" preparing these at cost for Dave's friends.

Stef remembers quite vividly the day the shirts arrived as they came just in time to deliver them at the Thanksgiving dinner at the U of A Hospital where a long table of Dave's friends and families had gathered to celebrate Thanksgiving just outside of the ICU. She walked into the hospital carrying a heavy box of T-shirts and met me at the doors where I escorted her to the gathering area. We opened the box together, and all of the guys with their unshaven faces each donned a T-shirt featuring a deep V, just like a team of sports players. For the first time in a while, there were smiles and laughter. "This is for you, Dave!" they exclaimed as they posed for the camera for a group shot, doing one of Dave's famous poses. Thanksgiving Dinner ensued, but before dinner was served, we went around the table and stood up to talk about what we were most thankful for, in celebration of Dave. Everybody would usually spend this time to talk about family and good health, but this year was different. Everybody was thankful for life even more than they knew. They were thankful for the technology of the hospital that was keeping our friend Dave alive; for the doctors and surgeons; and for the support network that sat directly in front of them. The T-shirts were just a small spot of light that night at the hospital, the beginning of a long journey of support that Dave still has.

The idea that Stef and I had prepared was eventually leaked when the pictures were posted, and the demand for these shirts became extraordinary. Over one hundred shirts were eventually made for guys and gals behind the idea—the campaign—that we had started in support of Dave not being able to shave for a while. Around ten friends grew very scraggly beards and kept them until Dave came out of his coma (with the exception of Dave's cousin, Chad Saleeby, who still has his!). *Bros and Babes* alike wore their shirts with pride and took pictures of themselves wearing them around the world. The T-shirts were a hit and we sold out of them almost instantly, raising $5,000 for the U of A Hospital Physiotherapy Department at the request of Dave and his family. It was literally the least we could do and made us feel like we were doing something good in the face of something so terrible. We still wear our shirts quite often, and whenever someone asks us to explain the slogan, we get to tell them the story of our pal Dave, and how he came back from the edge, stronger than before!

11. U OF A DENTAL STUDENTS COME THROUGH
Dr. Tammy Cameron, *DDS*

When I first met Dave, I thought he was funny, charismatic, and very charming. Brennan, my classmate and Dave's friend, told me of the accident at dental school and it was definite shock. I couldn't believe that someone like Dave, who was our age, was now fighting to hold onto his life. At the time we didn't know much of the extent or kind of journey Dave was about to go through, but we knew we had to do something, no matter how small, to show him and his family how important he is.

Brennan, Dave's brother Taylor, and their friends decided they were going to grow out their beards to show support, and make and sell T-shirts saying "Team David" and "Beards for Broborn" on them for 30 dollars each. Brennan and I were talking and thought, "Why don't we email the entire dental faculty, including seven dental and dental hygiene classes and the staff, to see if anyone else was interested in supporting the cause?" This was even more meaningful because Dr. Wayne Raborn, Dave's dad, was the former Dean of the Dental School and continues to have influence and teach dentistry at the U of A.

In a matter of minutes of sending the email, we were flooded with support. People wanted multiple T-shirts or simply wanted to donate to let the Raborns know they were all thinking of them. Our class then matched the donations from our class fund. The $1,100 in donations that we raised was added to the *Beards for Broborn* campaign, where a total of $5,000 was donated to the U of A Physio Department. The response was overwhelming and proved again what I already suspected of Dave: this is a really great guy who is surrounded by so much faith and love.

When I see Dave now, it seems surreal; his will to live and educate others inspire me still. And he didn't lose any of the charm that surrounded him from the first time I met him. I'm proud to know him and everything he is doing.

12. MUSINGS FROM AN RN
Adam Tuckwood, RN

I couldn't tell you the date if you asked me. I know it was September. And I know it was a nice day out. David and I had been talking earlier in that day about our P90X successes and failures, and other stuff you talk about with a good friend on a day that is like any other. He told me he was going for his daily (or his second daily) bike ride. David was an absolute workhorse at this point in our lives. He was probably in the best shape I had ever seen him, which—when you keep in mind we had played football together through our adolescence and he had gone on to play in university—is saying something. He worked non-stop, whether on his health or on his new business venture: a dating app idea with a twist (which was a great idea, because in today's world, the best way to meet a girl is to develop a dating app that makes you rich).

I can't remember if he asked me to join him on the ride, which he had done from time to time, or whether he was just telling me about his plan for the day, but the moment passed us by as quickly as you would nod to a friend from work at the mall, and with equally as much thought put to it. He sent me a picture an hour or so later of his bike that I had helped him fix up, casting a long *riderless* shadow of his bike across an early fall prairie landscape, with the caption "Ghost ridin' the whip!"... Something that at the time was just a cool picture but later haunted me. Neither of us were aware of the impact this particular bike ride would have on David's life, my own, and indeed everyone who had known him and would come to know him over the next year.

52

This story, like most in the real world, is neither all sad nor all happy, nor inspirational, nor shameful, nor devastating nor triumphant, but rather a gentle mix of all of those. Unlike telling a story in the pub to friends over a pint, I will not be able to gauge your response to the different aspects of the story and change my telling to suit whatever mood is needed. So I will do my best to not dwell on the harder parts of the story any longer than necessary, or to be too hilarious (which admittedly will be difficult for me, despite what my friends may tell you).

It was some time around 10:30 at night when I got a call from my good friend Brennan. An odd time to get a call from him, but not unheard of. When I answered the phone, I could tell there was something wrong; his tone wasn't his normal relaxed, laid-back tone. He told me that David had been in an accident and that he was in the hospital. He had fallen off his bike and needed to be taken to the emergency department. I am ashamed to admit that I didn't take it very seriously at the time. I was a nurse in the very hospital that David was in, and as many healthcare professionals will tell you, I had (and continue to have) a tendency to assume the health problems of those around me are less serious than the ones I see daily (which often is the case; however, as my wife will tell you, this isn't always the most helpful attitude for those feeling unwell).

I worked an evening shift the next day and had decided that I would go check on David before my shift, have a good laugh with him about however he had managed to hurt himself, and then continue on with my workday.

I woke up the next morning and headed to work. On my way in, I received word that they had needed to send David to surgery and that he was in the Neuro ICU. This raised my concern a little, but I didn't know what kind of surgery, and I told myself going to an ICU post-surgery isn't out of the ordinary if he had to be intubated. In hindsight, I was probably already in denial at this point. I arrived at work early and spoke to my manager about the situation. As it turned out, she had known David as well; Dave and I had both gone to school with her kids. She was shocked to hear the news, but I assured her that everything was okay and that after my visit I would be back in time to start my shift. She looked at me silently and asked if I was sure. I said I was, and that I'd rather be working. She agreed to my request, and I left with a forced smile to go visit my friend.

I have known David for most of my life. We played sports together, had class together, chased girls, drank beers, partied, worked out from our early teens until our early adulthood. David and I had stayed in touch and remained close friends through his years in Calgary playing football and going to school at the University of Calgary. He was as close to family as a friend could be.

David was always a good student and never got into much trouble that wasn't in good fun. That's not to say that he never got into any trouble, or that those situations weren't sometimes due to some less-than-wise decisions on his part. Being David's friend had always provided me with many an entertaining story. David had a knack for getting himself into, and out, of all kinds of ... lets call them ... "situations":

- He'd thrown a few large parties when his parents were away. And I mean *large*: 400 plus people, I would guess. His parents would always find out, but he and his brother would always have the house back in order before they arrived home.

- Late one night, David called me and said he needed help getting his parents' S.U.V. out of a bit of a tricky spot. He had gotten it stuck trying to impress a girl from work. And despite the somewhat violent manner in which he had gotten it stuck, he cleaned it up and his parents never found out (until now perhaps; sorry, Dave).

- One time in Grade 9, I beat David in the 100-metre dash at the school track meet. This story doesn't really fit in here; I just really wanted to tell it. Because it was awesome.

I have typed a half dozen or more of these stories, and then erased them. There are a lot of great stories I could tell, but they are not the one I started here, nor the ones you want to hear. My only real point in these little asides is that I had always known David to get himself into trouble, and I had always known him to get himself out as well. I saw no reason why this would be any different. Soon enough, this would be another story we could laugh about.

When I got down the stairs and began walking toward the unit I had been told David was on, there was no way I could have guessed how the next several hours, let alone several months, would go.

I remember the next ten minutes more vividly than almost anything in my life, for better or for worse. As I walked closer to the unit where David was supposed to be, I could see a few people I recognized. They looked up at me as I walked toward them. I smiled and waved. They did not respond. I had to move to the side to let a couple of porters and nurses rush by with a patient. I remember looking down at the person in the bed, and being grateful that my friend David wasn't as unlucky as this person. Looking into the face of this person, I couldn't imagine being where they were.

I looked back up as the bed passed me and waved again at my friends, and again they didn't respond. Because they weren't looking up to see me coming down the hall. They were looking up to see something else. It wasn't until the few friends I could see turned into a small group, then a couple dozen of people I knew, poking their heads around the corner, looking toward me but not at me, that I realized what was happening. I turned expecting to see David behind me. *But he wasn't there.*

And then when I turned back, the crushing reality hit me: David *was* behind me, but he had just passed me. He was in the bed. I had looked directly into his eyes and not known him as my lifelong friend. He had been two feet from me, and I had looked at him and away, without even recognizing him. Before I had a chance to catch up and look again at my friend, he, his bed and his nurses, all of his monitors and IVs, all disappeared behind the double mechanical doors of the Neuro ICU.

I turned back to the grim faces of David's friends staring after him as I had been doing. Before I had a moment to gather myself or speak to any of them, Mrs. Raborn and Dr. Raborn (affectionately referred to as Poppa Doc by David and many of us) were walking by. I can't remember if it was David's mom or dad who took my arm, but they asked me to come with them. They were going into a family conference with the surgeons, and they wanted me to be present for it.

At this point I really had no idea what was going on. I had been told only what I have said so far, and even though I now believed that it must be more serious than what I had initially hoped, I was in no way prepared for what I was about to walk into.

In my profession, I had become familiar with difficult family conversations. I had worked palliative care, chronic illness, and at this time was working in a group to help people with their end-of-life plans. I had been around the "family conference" table many times. But I had not been around this table. This table—though called the same thing, used for the same purpose, and by the same people—this table was completely foreign to me.

We walked into the room. Besides David's parents, it was Pastor Rita Penner, Lorne Penner and me. I sat at the farthest edge of the table. It was me on one end, then the Raborns, the Penners and finally the surgeon and his fellows on the opposite end.

The dull fluorescent lights hummed as we settled into our chairs and silence fell in upon us. The surgeon looked at the Raborns with a soft but serious gaze. He said although the surgery had gone well, he was not optimistic about David's chances for recovery.

The surgeon saying that he was not optimistic about David's chance of recovery hit me square in the chest. Not ten minutes earlier I had been walking down the stairs to visit my friend and laugh at whatever boneheaded predicament he had gotten himself into this time. I had been prepared to tell him that while he was in the hospital, I would come hang out when I could. If he had to stay a little while, maybe he'd come up and see where I worked before he got discharged home.

I was not prepared for this.

At first, I couldn't even understand the surgeon's words in context to the situation. Then my brain started putting his sentence together in my head, as if it had to relearn each of the words used and then figure out how they related to one another. I remember trying to rationalize it into meaning something other than what it had obviously meant.

This was the first of many times David's parents blew me away. I am sure I will mention this many times in my telling, but the strength these two had throughout this awful event was inspiring to say the least. Don't get me wrong: there were cracks in the pottery. There were hard days, and weeks; I would be lying if I said it didn't show more at some times than at others. But in the end, they were the very definition of bending but not breaking. They were the image of unconditional and unwavering love. And for this, I think they will always hold my respect and admiration.

The news we received at that table obviously struck them hard as well. I can't remember if anyone cried at this point. I can remember Mrs. Raborn tightening her grip on the hand of Pastor Rita. And I remember staring blankly at the surgeon. I can remember my mouth as dry as dust and the cool silence that often follows receiving unwelcome news.

David had suffered a very serious brain injury. They had to remove a large portion of his skull to relieve the pressure that was building due to the pooling of blood. He was being ventilated and was on medications to keep him asleep, and to keep his heart functioning at a level that would support his body but not so high as to do any more damage. The surgeon didn't expect him to last through the day. After some pressing from Dr. Raborn, the physician gave him a reluctant 50% chance of making it to the next day.

The Raborns held themselves very well though all of this. They always asked pertinent and important questions, and processed the information in a way that I have seen very few people capable of doing. And in those first few moments, when I was still reeling, they showed me what the strength I was going to need to have in the coming months looked like.

When we left the room, Mrs. Raborn asked me to go visit David on my own before they would let anyone else in to visit him. They wanted me to be able to prepare people for what they would see. I was happy to do this to help take some of the burden off the family, and though this role grew over the next several months to something I could have never anticipated, these first few hours were the worst of it.

I had no idea what to expect. Although I had done some work with people who had gone through brain surgery due to trauma before, it had never been at such an acute point. I rang into the unit and they opened the double automatic doors. The unit was organized in a U-shape. I came in at the top of one side of the U; David was around the horn of the U on the other side. In the middle of the U was the nursing station, desk, and medication room. So when I walked in, I had no clear eye line to David. In order to keep the intracranial pressure low, the environment in the Neuro ICU is dark and quiet. I asked at the desk where he was and they pointed me in the direction of the bed where David was lying. I walked to the foot of the bed and looked down at him. He was just as unrecognizable as he had been when he rolled by me in the hallway. He lay motionless. There was a multitude of tubes coming out of everywhere and going every which way. His head was completely wrapped in gauze. His face was very bruised. He was intubated and sedated. I had known this coming in. I had seen it before. But it is much different when it is someone you've known for years lying in that bed before you.

I took his hand and stood beside the bed. I told him that he had to make it through this, and that I knew he could do it. Then I cried. I am not honestly sure how long I was in there that first time. I don't really remember walking out. I can't remember to whom I spoke first. I know I spoke to the large group eventually. And although we were at first filing in two or three at a time, we eventually entered in two large groups because the nurses couldn't believe how many people had shown up for him; they wanted everyone in to visit and then to leave him to rest. Everyone responded a little differently to seeing David the first time. Many cried; some just stared; some spoke to him; a few people even became a little faint. Two, including one of his football teammates at university, actually fainted. We all left the room drained.

The stages of grief are an odd thing. How people manage difficult situations varies greatly, but in a room that large, filled with people who all had experienced the same terrible event, I had a unique opportunity to see many different methods. After leaving David's bedside the first time, I had kept myself composed as I went in with other people to prepare them for what they would see. I had done my best to stay strong, and I remember thinking that I had been handling it better than many of the people around me. A ridiculous thing to think for many reasons. What is "handling these things better"? Is there even such a thing? I came to realize in the days and months that followed the truth in how people deal with grief, and that there are few ways that are better or worse if we are being honest with ourselves. And in my thoughts of how well I was handling things, I had not been truthful with myself: in many ways, despite all my training and background, I was handling it far less appropriately than those around me. One of the greatest lessons David helped me learn through this was to feel your emotions as they come. Don't hold them back or refuse to acknowledge them; don't battle to keep them hidden ...

because it is a battle you will lose, and you will only exhaust yourself in the fight.

I began to learn that lesson that very morning. At some point, I realized I had not gone up for work yet, and that I should probably go and tell my boss that I might be a little late (I still had it in my head that I would be able to work. *Silly Adam.*) As if she knew, my manager came around the exact same corner I had walked around when David had rolled by me earlier. Gail had known me at this point for close to a decade through sports and work. She had actually spent some time working on the very unit that David now lay in his chemically-driven rest. I walked away from the group, some 50 yards or more, and met her. I opened my mouth to explain what had happened and to ask if it were okay if I was a little late, but nothing come out. No noise at all. I had choked on my words before I could get them out. I think my heart knew what my brain was trying to avoid, and it wouldn't let me pretend that I was stronger than this anymore. She looked at me knowingly, a calm gentle smile, took me around the shoulders, and I began to cry—"sob" is probably more appropriate. Gail took me to the side around a corner, draped her arm around my shoulders, and just let me cry. She had already called down to the unit to check on me, and the staff there had given her some indication of how I was managing. Before I could compose myself to say anything, she told me she had already gotten rid of my next several shifts and that I needed to be with my friend and to take care of myself. She didn't even give me the option, and I can't thank her enough for that. She was a great representation of a true and caring leader. It was a truly humbling and vulnerable moment for me (and anyone who knows me will tell you that vulnerability is something I avoid vigorously), and she treated it with the utmost respect.

Gail returned to her workday and I back to David's pack of supporters. Team David. My phone rang and texts rolled in for days after this as people heard the news. We had made it clear to everyone that if people wanted updates, they should come to me so that people trying to find out how David was progressing wouldn't overwhelm the family.

I decided to start a group on Facebook so I could provide mass updates that people could see at their own convenience. The group was called *"David Raborn, Updates and Prayers."* And this is was the first update that I gave to the group (complete with all the spelling errors that I am sure I have become famous for):

> *The Story as it stands today is as follows. On Thursday David was on a bike ride when at some point he attempted to lift his bike over an obstruction on the road and his front wheel became detached. He went over his handlebars and hit his head. He was found awake and was able to tell what happened as well as the phone number of his parents. On arrival to the hospital his situation took a turn and it was determined that he had a brain injury. He was rushed to the U of A and went straight into surgery. Since this point David has had a second surgery, the bone on the right side of his head removed, is sedated and intubated and one of his pupils is not reacting to light. As of this morning things are taking steps in the right direction. The pressure in his head has come down and*

thy have decreased his sedation. Some people have been lucky enough to see him move a little too. His pulse was quite high but is in now in normal ranges, and the pupil that was not reacting to light has gotten smaller but is still not reacting. He is however reacting to pain. These are all steps in the right direction. I know all his family is very appreciative of all the support they have been getting and they want to make sure you all knew that. I will put more here as I find out and encourage you to do the same. Unfortunately, due to him being in the ICU the Nurses have requested that the amount of visitors be minimal. They only asked this due to being blown away by the amount of people that showed up to support David. But if anyone has any questions please post them here and myself or someone else will do our best to help you out. Keep David in your prayers. I know he's feeling them and they are helping. Thanks.

Within a couple of hours of starting the group, it had grown to over several hundred members. And it steadily grew as time passed. Up to over 700 members. Even today, it still sits well over 500. There are a lot of negative things that social media can produce and there are a lot of evils that come from it, but this little forum was such a great help to so many people, and the credit goes to all those people who participated, especially David's brother, Taylor. Over the months of his recovery, I posted many times about his ups and downs and received many messages and questions. It became a place for people to share fond memories, and to console each other when times called for it. It also had its drawbacks. Mixing high emotion into any situation can often result in things being done, or said, when they shouldn't have, or in things being misinterpreted, and this group was not exempt from that. There were even times when I considered shutting it down, but I am thankful I never did. It helped far more than it hurt.

I also had a group chat with a group of guys who had all known David well, and we supported one another a lot in these early days. If no other positive came of this terrible event (other than David's recovery, of course), it allowed a group of young men to learn to express their friendship and love with each other on a regular basis. When you get so close to losing someone, it really shines a light on the ridiculousness of us being worried about showing each other affection. It's been a great thing. (On a side note: I love you guys.)

Anyway, I digress; I'm sure you all don't care about my "bromances," so I will continue with the story.

Over the next several weeks, we watched David slowly get better and better, day-by-day. He was eventually moved out of the ICU, woke up, and could communicate in some fashion, although at this time it was still not overly clear, in writing or sometimes even verbally (although to be fair David's writing wasn't ever too clear if I remember correctly—just kidding, buddy!). It seemed that David was out of the woods and that, even if slowly, he was recovering. They had even replaced the bone they had removed from his skull.

It was around this time as well that Stef Williams and Kevin Meleskie (with minimal help from myself) set up *Beards For*

Broborn. Broborn was one of David's nicknames. The name *Broborn* came from a very intricate and complex method our friends had of devising nicknames for one another. I'll do my best to describe it, but its complicated, so don't feel bad if you get lost along the way: we would take the first few letters out of your last name and replace them with "Bro." Yes, that's it. So Tuckwood became Browood, Dehod became Brohod, and Raborn became Broborn. (He actually got this nickname from Scott McKenna, or Brokenna, David's teammate from U of C and the originator of this complex system.) If you have to put the book down to mull this over in your head a bit, it's okay. I'll wait here.

Back? Okay, good. So *Beards for Broborn* was basically the act of us not shaving until David had improved. (We wouldn't even let the nurses shave David's awful Movember moustache for a while, but one of them had mercy on him and took it off over a night shift). They organized to sell shirts as well and raised a fair bit of money that after his recovery, David was able to donate to some of the people who helped him get back to us. It was all pretty cool.

Since David was in the hospital over Thanksgiving, and the Raborns were at the hospital a great majority of the time, it was decided that we would have Thanksgiving in the hospital with them. I believe it was Leah Karch who organized most of it and who cooked this massive turkey! It was huge! Everyone brought something, and we set up a long table and all sat along it. I can't remember how many people were there; I want to say around 20, but what I do know for sure is that it was a pretty special event for the Raborns and for those of us who were able to take part. We were even able to provide a meal for a few other families who were stuck in the hospital. It was a pretty good day, or as good as it could've been under the circumstances.

Shortly before a trip the boys took, which David was supposed to be a part of, I had a dream. Now I know this sounds very corny and straight out of Hollywood, but I dreamed I was at a party, having a good time, and at some point I decided to leave. As I walked out of the house and down the sidewalk, I came up to David. It seemed he had been waiting for me. He was completely fine, as if nothing had happened at all. We walked down the sidewalk in a calm clear summer night, hanging out as we often did. At some point we decided to lie down on a patch of grass and stare into the night sky. We didn't speak. Just gazed into the never-ending space. After some time, without looking at him, I said, *"You have to make it."* There was a moment or two of silence, and he replied, *"I will."* And then I woke up. I felt pretty confident after that night, for a little while at least.

Shortly after our trip, David hit his second major bump. Over the course of several days, David's symptoms began to slowly get worse again. It was his mother who noticed first. He was slightly less awake and was having difficulty doing the things he was able to do only days earlier. Upon further investigation, it was discovered that David had begun to bleed in his brain again, and the pressure was building up. It was as if he had another head injury. This resulted in more surgeries and another trip back to the ICU.

His recovery from this was not nearly as smooth.

I had thought the most difficult part of this ordeal was to see the friend I had been talking to only the day before suddenly in a coma with a 50% chance of making it to the next day. I had known that the recovery would be long and slow, but I was sure that would be the hardest part. Watching my good friend slowly slide back from the landmarks he had been achieving in his recovery easily proved to be just as difficult, and at times, perhaps more-so.

The light that was David was slowly fading with each return to the ICU, each day passing without any improvements. David's GCS (which stands for Glascow Coma Scale, a method used by healthcare professionals to determine the level of consciousness of a patient that in an otherwise unaffected patient sits at a 15 of a total 15), was often around a 9, and sometimes an 8 depending on the day. A score of 8 or below is considered comatose. David will tell you that he doesn't remember much, if anything, from this time, and I believe it. It was all too often that I'd see him looking at me and hardly recognize the man behind the eyes.

I don't remember when it occurred, but at some point Dave acquired C. diff (also know as Clostridium difficile), a superbug that is common in hospitals. It is not uncommon for the normal person to have this bacterium in their system; however, it is usually kept at bay by the many other bacteria that we have in our bowels. Sometimes a patient can be exposed to a particularly strong strain, and it becomes an issue; alternatively a patient who has been given strong antibiotics can have the good bacteria in his gut killed off, leaving the much more durable C. diff bacteria plenty of room to grow. The unfortunate result of this on the patient is similar to a stomach bug you might get from bad food. It can last for weeks and can cause severe dehydration. Pair this with David's lack of movement and decreased nutrition, and the result was David losing huge amounts of weight. As I said earlier, David was in great shape. And it's a good thing too—I'm not sure he would have made it otherwise. David lost at least 70 pounds during that time. He was a shell of what he was. He went from being at a point where he could speak slow sentences and write messy messages to hardly being able to move at all. Some days he wouldn't do more than open his eyes. He was literally skin and bones.

Throughout this entire time, Mrs. Raborn hardly left his side. She kept watch on him and more than once noticed changes before the medical staff did. This made it even more difficult to convince her to take some time to rest herself. Despite many of us doing all we could to try to help her get the rest she needed, she was determined to be there for David when he needed her. Many times when I thought she must be on the brink of exhaustion, she continued (with Dr. Raborn's help I'm sure) to find whatever she needed to keep going. I know there were many, many nights when I and their family friend Mrs. Mador (Janet) did all we could to try to get Mrs. Raborn to go for a rest. We rarely won. Mrs. Raborn would not leave David's side unless she wanted to. And she is without a doubt, in my mind, one of the biggest factors in David's recovery.

Yet one more time the Raborns blew me away.

Another testament to David and the Raborns was the volume and persistence in help they had from the people in their lives. There is no way I could possibly give an adequate depiction of all of the amazing gestures of love and friendship I saw given to the Raborns through all of this.

I'd like to tell you I never lost hope that David would recover. I would like to say that through all of this, I always knew that David would bounce back. But that is not case.
It was hard for me to watch David slide. It was equally difficult to watch his family deal with his decline.

The holidays are a difficult time in hospitals. Perhaps because it's a time of year we usually dedicate to good times with families and friends, when things are so obviously not a happy time, the holidays can make us feel so much lower than we were before. I can't imagine what that Christmas must have been like for the Raborns. David is a very close friend of mine, and it was difficult for me. It must have been truly draining for his family. And although he can't remember it, I'm sure it was awful for David, too.

As the friend or family of someone in the hospital, you often feel unsure of what to do—how to act, what to say, when to be around, when to let them rest. It is such a foreign and uncomfortable environment for most of us. Many people feel the need to speak more slowly to the patient or to talk to them as if they are helpless or a child. Some have a hard time with the interaction at all and either avoid it altogether or visit without any real interaction. I did my best to keep it as natural as I could, speaking or acting as if David were in the same state as he had been prior to the accident. I wasn't entirely successful, to be honest. When speaking to someone for several months without any, or least very much, response, it is difficult to maintain the same air that we had before. I tried to remind myself that David was in there, and he'd probably go mad if I came and talked to him everyday as if he were my four-year-old nephew. Before the accident, David loved listening to me talk to him for hours and hours without pause. Some might say it was his favourite thing (at least that's what I told myself. In reality I suppose that may have not been the case). So sometimes when I visited all I did was say hi, hang out a bit, and then take off. The farther away David seemed to slip from us, the more difficult carrying that air of relaxed conversation and interaction became.

The group of guys who I talked with most often were all dealing with David's condition in their own way. There were those among us who would say without fail that he would get better any day, and there were those who felt less optimistic. I had seen many people go down the path David appeared to be traveling. I had become unavoidably aware of where that path would most likely come to an end. On one of our nights at the pub, the topic came up. I had been avoiding the subject, to be honest. I didn't want to talk to our friends about how David may not get better. But I feared it was more than that: that he would *likely* not get better. That how he was on that day would likely be the best he would ever be, and if he lived at all, it wouldn't be at all the way we had known him. That night was not nearly as light-hearted as our evenings out normally were. I felt that it was my job to make sure that my friends were prepared for what may be coming. I can't think of any other time I was so grateful for being wrong.

I think I had come to grips with what I thought was the inevitable future: that if David made it out of the hospital, he wouldn't make it out as the David I grew up with in any way. I have a theory of what happened next. It has little to do with medicine. I grew up with David. He and our friend Brandon got me hooked on hip-hop music during junior high school (much to my wife's dismay). We had shared sports, weekends, traveling (including a road trip where David ended up wedged in with five guys' bags for the majority of the trip)—we were even in a musical in high school together. So I got to know him pretty well. And David had a habit of being very, if not overly, hard on himself. If David made a mistake on the court or the field, he'd get down on himself pretty hard. And until he decided to pull himself out of it, there wasn't much to be done about it. I can still remember David pulling his shirt over his head because of a bad pass in basketball or a missed set in volleyball. Once I saw that, I knew we had lost him for a bit. But once he cleared his head and got back to it, he'd come back the same awesome kid and teammate we knew him to be. I think that being knocked down by something he had no control over, after doing all that hard work to recover the first time, had sent him into a tailspin, and he had pulled his shirt up over his head for a bit.

After Christmas, his mom really started pushing him to progress. They were looking at rehabilitation programs, and we all wanted him to be stationed in the one within our city as opposed to the one about an hour and half away in Ponoka, Alberta. But to do that, David had to show some progress. He had to show some more steady improvement. His mother and the rehabilitation team worked with him a lot in those days. But, in my opinion, it was when David dug his feet in again that things really started to happen. Slowly he began to move more and respond more. Whatever fog he

72

was in started to clear, and I could see more and more "David" behind his eyes.

We had his birthday and got him some new kicks and a nice hat, because you've got to look good to get better; that's just science. We played poker, and he didn't only win, but he booed our good friend, Gray, in the process. It was the improvement we were all praying for, and it was happening.

David's parents worked so hard with him, and David had good days and bad days, but he was starting to progress. I remember the day of his evaluation. I remember how nervous everyone was. How desperately we wanted to make sure the evaluators would see what we saw. That they would see he was still in there and that he wanted to come back. I wasn't there for the evaluation. I never heard anything about how it went, what they tested, how he did. I did, however, hear a few days later, that whatever it was that David did, he did a great job, and he had gotten into the world-renowned rehabilitation centre of the Glenrose Hospital. David was working really hard again. And his progress was showing it. I was so excited for him. He had done such a great job. His parents were also feeling great, and I don't know they appreciate how much of an effect they had on his success; they were perhaps too close to appreciate it. But as much as David wouldn't have made it without his own determination, strength, and drive, he wouldn't have made it far without all of their love and support either. I say again, their strength and perseverance through all this was amazing. They had their weak moments; we all did. But they were, and still are, some of the strongest people I have ever seen when faced with such a horrific event.

Before I knew it, David was gone. He had left my hospital and had been moved to the Glenrose. I had visited David almost every day for months. And just like that he was ... gone. It was weird. I was so happy he was doing better, but I also missed being able to go check in on him, to say, "What's up?", and to see how he was doing that day. I had been a lot of people's resource for updates, and all at once, I was as detached as everyone else. I didn't like that. I didn't like it at all.

That was until I visited him at the Glenrose for the first time.

It was a week from when he had been moved, the longest it had been between my visits by a long shot since he had had his accident. This is one of my favourite moments and favourite stories to tell. Mrs. Raborn had told me his unit and room number, and I was on my way to go see him. The last time I had seen David, he was struggling to speak, was moving much better than he had been, but was still very emaciated from months of bed rest. I walked onto the unit, down the main hallway, and bumped into a nurse I had gone to school with. After a little small talk, I asked him where I could find Dave.

He said, "I think I just saw him walking down the hall to his room, last door on the left."

I looked at him little puzzled. "You must be confused," I said. "David just got here this week; he isn't walking yet."

He looked back at me. "David Raborn? No, that's him. Last door on the left."

74

I walked down the hall in disbelief. Knocked on his door, walked in. There in the bed was David. He turned his head to me.

"Hey, Tuck," he said, clear as day.

This is the first time I had heard David acknowledge me by name in months. He was moving around, talking. In the week since I had seen him last, he had improved by an amount I didn't even think was possible. A mere couple of months earlier, I wasn't sure he was going to make it at all. And there he was, killing it. We had a conversation. It was slow, and not super in-depth, but we talked. Back and forth. I didn't stay long because Dave was tired from walking "like a boss," so he needed some rest. I was absolutely floored when I got back to my car. It didn't seem possible. And yet there he was.

For a few weeks I was still really hesitant to believe he was really getting better, expecting a setback anytime. But every time I saw him, he was killing it more and more. Our conversations were getting better and better. They were mostly about food—but if you hadn't eaten in seven months, I suspect that would be on *your* mind, too. Although it changed from time to time, the big things Dave told me he wanted was a Five Guys burger or an Arby's sandwich, and lemon meringue pie—solid choices, I think we can all agree.

David kept improving and improving. A large group of us went to a class that would help to prepare us for what may be on the horizon for him as he continued outside of the hospital. It was an excellent program that did us all a lot of good. And then before you know it, David was home. Yup. *Home.*

After months and months of extreme turmoil, he was home. Back in his own house. With his family. His parents. His grandma who he calls Namma (a wonderful woman, who helped hold down Dave's home when his parents were in and out to visit him in the hospital so much. She's another cornerstone in the strength of the family). He was hanging out with his brother when he was in town. Making bad jokes. Improving everyday. Eventually going back to work! Driving! Working out! Through his improvement, David moved a little more slowly, but one day a good friend of ours, Danny Reimer, a personal trainer who was helping Dave "get back to it" (as Dave once put it to me) said that David had picked up a skipping rope and just started going! He was performing doubles, crossovers, and everything. The kid just kept shocking me every time I saw him.

A few years later I was getting further education in intensive care, where I eventually went to work, and found that when it came to brain injuries, David repeatedly had the worst-case scenario. And he repeatedly beat it. *He was the outlier.* And thank God for that.

If you met David today, you wouldn't have any idea about the things he went through. You wouldn't know that he was on death's doorstep more times over a couple months than most of us will be in our entire lives, God willing. You would see an extremely kind and thoughtful man. My wife, who met David several years after this ordeal, absolutely loves him and jumps at any chance we have to hang out with him. He volunteers to coach basketball, he works, he hangs out with the boys, and he goes on the odd date. On one September day, the world tried to take him from us. But with a little help from his friends, a lot of help from his family, and the determination of a driven man, he came back.

He pulled everyone around him closer to each other and to him. He made us all appreciate one another, and he helped us all tell each other about that appreciation instead of leaving it unsaid. A community came around to support David and help make him grow strong again. But in the end, it was he who made us stronger.

I enjoy writing. I do it often—nothing world-changing, but just as an outlet. This has been by far one of the most difficult things that I have ever put to paper. Remembering some of these events has brought me to tears. There were days, and weeks, when I couldn't write because I knew what was coming next, and I didn't want to remember it. If you take nothing more from my small section of this story, I hope you take two things in particular. One, there are few things that are impossible when you have the support of friends and family. And two, tell the people around you how much you care for them. Leave no doubt. We shouldn't need terrible things to teach us to be open with each other. Caring is not weakness; it is strength.

And in that spirit, I'll leave you by telling everyone how much I love my family, my friends, and my wife. And thank you, David, for teaching me that I should be saying it more often.

13. HELLO, DAVE
Julian Marchand

Hello, Dave. Here is what you missed. You missed saving my life.

Before your accident, I was in a deep depression. I felt alone, unfulfilled, and without purpose. This isn't the first time that I felt this way; I have been struggling with suicidal intentions my entire life. But this time was different. I was away from my family and disconnected from the people who kept me grounded to reality.

People talk about depression as if it is something that can be overcome with sheer will power. That only the weak-minded are the ones who succumb to it. This could not be further from the truth. I cannot speak for everyone who has a mental illness or who goes through a tough time and has decided that taking his or her life is *their only choice*. That complete nothingness seems like a better alternative to the unrelenting darkness. It swallows you like a black hole, snuffing out the light and creating a self-fulfilling prophecy set in motion by one's own inability to accept even a semblance of hope. That was me.

The problem was that people would misunderstand my pain for arrogance. Assume that I was a jerk—narcissistic, chauvinistic, self-absorbed, selfish, ignorant, spineless, hopeless, pathetic, a waste of human life. Or at least that's how it felt to me. I would constantly assume the worst of others—that they hated me, judged me, and mocked me. It became a prison of my own creation, forged from opinions that may or may not have existed.

It swallowed me like an endless slab of wet concrete.

Everyday I sunk just a little bit further until I stopped hearing or seeing anything, and was left with only my internal voice. A voice in my head that said, *"You will never be anything. People hate you because you deserve to be hated; you aren't worthy of love. You're pathetic, weak, foolish and stupid, a waste of human life with nothing to provide anyone. Hopeless... you belong here, you deserve to suffer."*

That's how I felt every day, every week, every month for about a year before your accident. Prior to that, it had been grade 12 for about three years into university, and before that it was from grade 5 until I moved to Cochrane. The majority of my life has been spent hating myself, truly believing that I had nothing to offer and that my immediate world would be better off without my inconvenient existence.

I was a dead man walking when you crashed your bike; I had nothing left to give and felt nothing. Joy was not a luxury of my life; self-loathing consumed my daily activities, to the point where I had emotionally checked out, similar to what you consider someone with no soul. Nothing fazed me. I knew my end date, and I knew my story. Honestly, those days were the least sad moments of my time in Edmonton. I was no longer sad.

And then I got a text from Phil.

You had been in a crash. I had no idea about the severity and so I called the hospital, where I was working as a bed manager at the time, and requested some information from a colleague. She told me that the ambulance had arrived at the scene and you would be arriving at the hospital ASAP.

I didn't even react. I finished my game of NHL with Kyle before heading to the hospital. I wasn't worried, nor was I impacted. I was just a warm body going to check on a friend. I still don't understand how I could have reacted the way that I did—emotionless, indifferent. For that I am sorry. I hope you know that I am the one who feels indebted to you and your family. All that I have and all that will be is a result of what happened, and this is how I recollect the events of your accident.

I arrived at the hospital and you were nowhere to be found. I asked my fellow co-workers to help me locate you, and I went up to the Neuro ICU. Arriving at the Neuro unit, I saw your mom; she was obviously distressed. I still had no idea what happened, but I knew at this moment, since you were in the neurological unit and since you were placed directly into surgery without going through emergency, you were in critical condition. At that moment, I met Lauren Dary and also really met your parents for the first time. Your mom was still as polite and caring as anyone I have ever met, even in the presence of such overwhelming adversity, and you father, in that moment, showed strength that will resonate within me for the rest of my life.

Your dad walked up to Lauren, your mother and I after speaking with someone on the medical staff. You could tell he was well informed about the severity of the injury and was providing as few details as possible. He mostly told us that you had a bad fall and they were going to take you for surgery to try to reduce the pressure on your brain. What I didn't know at the time was that your father had served in the military on a surgical team in the Vietnam War. I knew that he had a background in medicine because of his designation and career, but I did not understand the extent of it. Your father was rational, collected, and calm during the initial part of your accident. This is unbelievable to me because he would have an acute understanding of the severity and the outcome of this diagnosis, even though at this point all we knew was that you were getting the pressure relieved from your brain. To me that doesn't seem so bad; but if you had the knowledge base to understand the critical conditions that must be required for them to perform this type of procedure, then you would know it was life-threatening.

You were in the operating room and your father took your mother to get cup of tea; I think he did this because it provided a task, something tangible that she could do so she wasn't just sitting there stewing. Lauren Dary and I stayed behind and we let them know that if there were any new developments, we would come find them.

Across the lobby from Lauren and I were a mother and two children. They were frantic. They were on the same unit, which means that it probably wasn't the best news. Their doctor arrived, and I remember his temperament, his disconnected awkward stature. At first, I found this extremely off-putting; you always think that doctors are compassionate, caring, empathetic people—or at least you hope they are. This statue moseyed toward them and delivered his facts: the father had had a massive head trauma and it was unlikely that he would recover. I remember the screams from the two children, no older than 9 and 12. They were piercing.

I remember being upset by the entire situation. Why was the doctor presenting the news in front of these children and why was the mother allowing them to be there for this conversation? It was made worse by the mother who, instead of protecting the children, began to pile on. She asked what his chances were. When the doctor replied, "less than half," the children lost it. They began crying and were inconsolable. Instead of feeling sorry for the children I was infuriated by the mother, who seemed to have absolutely no concern for the impact that this conversation would have on her children for the rest of their lives.

She began to guilt the doctor and inquired as to what she should do now and whether they should be getting funeral plans in order. All the while the children were absolutely falling apart. She finally led them away and they disappeared into the darkness of the hallway. I never saw those children again.

I remember this story, Dave, because it is a stark contrast between your family and theirs; your father was a shield and your mother was a sword. Your father always received the information and would then explain all of the conditions and procedures in a manner that calmed everyone and kept their minds at ease. I have inquired since dating Lil, a registered nurse, about some of your procedures and some of the infections that you got. She says a lot of people die from all of the "hiccups" that you had throughout your recovery process. You know what's crazy? Speaking with your dad, you would never have felt like it was anything outside of standard process. He knew differently, of course, but he shielded everyone from the possibility of impending doom.

Your mom and dad re-joined Lauren and me, and we all chatted about anything and everything, making conversation out of the most mundane topics so that we could keep the silence at bay. Silence was the one thing that could crush the morale of your recovery; fortunately, the power of numbers and positivity never allowed for that negative silence to creep into our consciousness. That was the power of people: keeping the mind from wandering to a bad place, from the thoughts of despair and the worst-case scenarios, running the simulations about what should happen if, if, if... the funeral, the despair. No parent should bury their child who is only in his or her twenties.

Your doctor arrived, and he seemed just as disconnected at the one I had watched only moments before. He told us that they had relieved the pressure by removing a chunk of your skull, which allows for the brain to swell without causing additional damage. The next 48 hours would be the longest hours of your parents' lives, as the doctor informed us that if you were to survive that timeframe, you would have a chance at survival. Well, I'd have to say you made the most of that opportunity.

I can't remember who asked what your odds of surviving were, but that's irrelevant. Looking back, that entire question seems irrelevant now because there is no definite way to give any kind of certainty for that value. He could have said a 75% chance or a 1% chance; either way people decide how they are going to react to the perception of death. Do we panic like the family I had viewed just moments before? Do we writhe in despair? Bury ourselves in irrational optimism? Go into a state of shock and denial?

What happened next was a feat of strength, one that I didn't believe was possible, and a testament to years of hardship and character building that only comes from witnessing adversity. Mama Raborn began to cry, but your dad, who knows what the prognosis likely means for his son, did not; he maintains vigilance. He not only consoles his wife but also empowers us to believe that there is hope, and that wallowing in grief will not help Dave, nor will it help us. In that moment I witness the true measure of a man; it is a moment that I will remember until the end of my days. He was shield for everyone. That's your father: throughout the process he was a guardian, and I never saw anything dent, chink, ding, or penetrate that armour. Your father is a great man.

I knew I could be there for your family, that I could help take some of this burden, but I don't think it was because I was strong. I think it was because I was already broken and nothing could make me feel less whole. In time, I'd come to realize that even though I felt broken, maybe I could be fixed.

Over time I came to feel like a part of your family, in the sense that your mom, dad, and brother asked me for help if they needed anything; this connection, and seeing what setbacks did to them, changed my entire outlook on life. It took a long time for me to realize and change my mindset, but your parents didn't just help you back on your feet; they also showed me the strength of family. They showed me how losing a piece of that puzzle not only makes the family incomplete, but also fractures the strength of the unity. It is an irreplaceable bond, and your family helped me realize the impact and value that I can have on my own family. It gave me a new purpose.

I had to be up the next morning, So I headed home at around 4:00 AM. It didn't really faze me though, because I was used to going to bed late. Looking back on it now, the weird part was that I wasn't affected by the situation; I went home and slept. I slept well. I don't know if I was exhausted and didn't realize it, or if I was so disconnected from reality that I was unable to emotionally engage in the situation. Like a robot going though the motions, I had become no different than the doctor that night. Methodical, constant, cold, and lifeless.

The next morning I woke up and went through my daily routine. I went back to class and then stopped in to see Dave before heading to Foote Field for my football game that night. During that visit, the outpouring of positivity and support began, and I believe that those positive attitudes lifted your spirits. I know that they lifted mine.

Visiting you in the hospital became a relief for me. I would get away from football and the constant judgments that I felt faced me everyday and I would just be present. There was only something important to talk about: you. How you were doing and how people were holding up. My response was simple: I'd lie. I couldn't really tell people that I had been suffering from major bouts of depression and was planning on ending my life come January. That's not really a strong conversation starter. So I would choose to lie, put a smile on my face, and engage in conversation. People would constantly pour in, excited that you were alive but devastated at your condition.

The first weekend, when the U of C boys came up from Calgary, there was quite a stir; a handful of people came up to see you and lend their support. Unfortunately, some people couldn't handle the sight of your head and face … and I don't really blame them. The ICU area where you were being kept would normally only allow one or two visitors at a time. They had to make up a special procedure to allow four to six visitors into your room because they had never seen an outpouring of support like this before. People were lining up around the block (well, corner) to see you.

Adam Bunz finally got to go in and hang with your mom. She seemed pretty tired at this point, probably because she wasn't really sleeping and was trying to be the most southernly hospitable person in the building. This is a daunting task when there are 100 people visiting everyday at all different hours of the day. It got to the point where I came to see you and I found your mom sleeping in the "library," which was just a tiny room with some books. So I sat down with her and answered any questions people had until your mother woke up. The first thing she said was, "Oh, I must have shut my eyes for a moment there; I'm sorry. Julian, how are you?" Visiting with your mother always brought a smile to my face. There are very few people in this world that would apologize for taking a nap while their son is in the Intensive Care Unit. Your mom is one of those people, a true southern belle.

Anyways, I digress. Bunz walked into the ICU "all bright eyed and bushy-tailed," very excited to see you … and five minutes later I see a beet-red Adam Bunz being wheeled out of the hospital room with an ice pack on his back saying, " I'm FINE! I DON'T KNOW WHAT HAPPENED, BUT THIS IS RIDICULOUS. SERIOUSLY, I'm FINE!"

He had fainted at the sight of you. It was great, and this became a running joke every time Bunz would come visit. When one of the Schmidt boys saw you and fainted as well, people started making some quip about how we should make sure your room was wheelchair accessible.

Unfortunately, the reason for his fainting spell was no laughing matter. He saw your head, and fainted. I understand how someone could have had this reaction; I think that if I had had any empathy at that point (and wasn't as disconnected as a sociopath on Tinder) then I would have wept overtime when I saw your condition. It was graphic, and the stillness of your body was disheartening. You are one of the most joyful people I have ever known; you never stop moving and you always have a smile on your face, so to see your inanimate body laying on a bed with your eyes swollen shut and half of your skull crushed in was too much for some people to take.

Whether people were from North Carolina, Georgia, Lethbridge, Calgary, or Edmonton, you would hear them all telling stories in the lobby and at your bedside. People would chat for hours and hours and fill the hall with noise and happiness. Even though the entire ordeal should have been depressing, it wasn't. We would chat, reminisce, and laugh together. The stories brought joy to more than just the hospital; they were a retreat from my own life. They helped numb the unrelenting emptiness I was facing.

Coming to visit you gave me a sense of purpose. As I continued to come, I became a part of a community of people who were going through the same thing, and I no longer felt as if I were alone. It was an opportunity to forget my own problems. It became a therapeutic event for me and was always uplifting. You gave me purpose. That's the one thing that changed. One of the worst things that can happen to a person is to feel like they're isolated with no sense of self. To be completely alone. I was no longer that person.

Once you were able to receive visitors and leave your room, we would go to the atrium and sit around to talk. The room was filled with drinks and plants and provided a much more inviting area for the group of people to meet. The conversations all began the same over the course of the visits in the hospital. We would all get together and start talking to one another as if nothing had happened. People would try to engage you but during the first few months, the only responses we could get from you were in the form of blinking. If we were lucky, that is.

These times together were some of the most fun; we would sit around and talk. Talk about anything and everything. As the visits and the months continued, we were able to get smiles, laughs, and even the occasional word or two from you.

I have three very young siblings, and hearing you speak again was similar to hearing them speak for the first time; you always expect it to happen sometime, but until it does you never believe it will be real. You were never supposed to speak again, and when you finally did, it changed lives. Hope was carried on every syllable. Joy filled that atrium every time you visited it.

By January, you had recovered to the point where you were able to interact with visitors. We would have you sit up and play board games with us. You and I would play *Connect 4* for about 20-30 minutes before we called it a day. My mindset for these games has never changed from the first day that I met you: it's not about making you *feel* better; instead, it's always about pushing you to *be* better. So I never took it easy on you, not ever, and especially in the one-on-one basketball that we had often played at the U of C. I know this sounds cold, but as you began to express your emotions, you reacted naturally and on cue to times that you made a mistake. I enjoyed that the most, because it showed me you were still in there.

Your walking came in steps. We would first use supported harnesses to get you vertical and at a point where you would be able to support yourself. This was an amazing starting point because it allowed for the progression for the future.

Really though, I never think about any of the starting points. I just have moments with you. I had moments where we would play baseball with a balloon, or where we would match teams to the mascots for NCAA teams. There was even the time you made a quip about how it could snow in any month of the year. Even in June.

You: eating tater tots for the first time. It was the first time you were allowed solid food. You cried. It was very emotional. I had never heard someone say tater tots are amazing before. (Just kidding. They are amazing.) All I could do was worry about you choking, and I'm sure I wasn't the only one who was worried about that.

You had a tiny basketball net, and we would play horse on it. I still never took it easy on you, as I couldn't allow you to ever beat me at basketball. No excuses. I also never believed in changing the way I treated you because of your accident. If you beat me, then you earned the victory and everything you had been working toward was not for naught. *It was not for nothing.* If there is one thing I know about your rebirth, it is that you are the most stubborn person I have ever met.

All of my happiest memories in Edmonton were spent with you in either the hospital or at the Glenrose. It was a little selfish of me to think this at the time, but when you went home from long-term care, *that* was a most bittersweet day in my life. I had seen you emerge victorious from what seemed like an insurmountable obstacle. How selfish of me to think that I had lost the place where I felt the safest. I still to this day look for the things that have changed with you. Now that I see you less frequently, the changes are much more dramatic. The daily adventures made it seem almost unchanged over the course of your recovery even though you had excelled in ways most physicians thought impossible.

14. THE WINK
Julian Marchand

Right when you were beginning to communicate, there was a moment that shook me. It shook everyone, in fact. It was a very normal day; I was skipping early film session in order to hang out with you, and we both know how much I loathed watching film. You had recently begun tracking people's movements with your eyes. You mom was ecstatic because she truly believed that this was a sign of cognitive function. I was less convinced, but I felt like there was no reason to not be outwardly optimistic about the situation.

You were unable to move your head, though there was the occasional time you would blink and respond to instructions or commands. Unfortunately, these responses could easily be deemed as "coincidental" by the associated medical staff, which I could totally understand. Your mother would ask you 100 questions in a row, asking you to blink once if you understood. Well, eventually you have to blink, so I understood why the doctors were skeptical, but I also understood why your mother was enthusiastic.

She never broke that character, and over time I realized it wasn't an act. It must be where you got your unrelenting positivity from. It is a wonderful trait; both you and your mother bring instantaneous happiness to the room when you walk in. The mood always seems to lift when you are around, and that didn't change even when you were unable to communicate. If your eyes were open, happiness filled the room.

We chatted for about 45 minutes, and I always tried to keep you informed with the latest gossip (I know how much you like the gossip). Mostly I would tell you about football, about my family, about our friends, about school. You loved when I talked about school though; you learned all about the different types of soil and how they interact with plants. You loved it so much that you would almost always become over-stimulated and fall asleep (or at least that's how I would interpret it).

On the day you began to really communicate, we didn't talk about soil. There were a lot of people who were coming in and out of the room, and with your eyes, you would constantly track the person moving. The doctors would claim that this is an instinctual response to stimulus and that it does not signify cognitive function. Regardless, I found it amazing to watch, because for a long time, even when your eyes were open, *there was no one home.* At this point in the recovery, I felt like any function was a positive sign of progress.

Finally, I had to head out to practice. On my way out I said, *"Hey Dave, give me a wink!"* and I winked at you. Almost instantaneously, you winked with your right eye back at me. I was stunned, but at that moment I realized that you would make it, and that your mom was right. *You were in there*; you just had to find your way back. Some points in your recovery process stick with me the most. This was one of the biggest ones, because it was the first time that you responded on command.

However, you weren't able to wink again for a couple of months. The doctors said for a long time that it was an uncontrolled reaction to my stimulus, but I thought that to be illogical. Especially because every time I tried to get you to wink in the future you would blink. I always equated it to the kid who sinks a half-court shot on his first attempt: they always have the intent to perform that action, but it is highly unlikely that, based on the circumstances, they would be able to repeat it at will.

You were in pretty rough shape. For the next countless months, I would refer to your brain as Windows 95: we would see that you were processing the information, but it was a struggle for you to complete the command. It is a testament to your resilience that you were able to come back from such unrelenting adversity. You did, and every victory you reached showed me that through the power of will and positive thinking, anything can be accomplished. There is nothing greater than the power of the spirit. Belief in one's self is the only way to unlock that power. Thank you for providing me with the key.

[*As a wonderful update, I'd like to share that I traveled this Summer (of 2017) to Julian and Lil's outstanding wedding. I couldn't be happier for my friends and wish them both the very best.*]

15. THANKSGIVING IN THE HOSPITAL
Leah Karch

When David's friends heard about the accident and the critical nature of his injuries, I think most of us were in disbelief. The thought that he could be taken away from us was horrible. So we did what any friends would do: we camped out at the hospital. People would go when they could and at any given time there was always a group congregated outside of David's unit. We would reminisce and talk for hours. We wanted to be there for David, and his family, and each other.

My husband Dylan and I had a seven-month-old baby girl at the time, and we brought her with us every time we came. She became something of a symbol of hope and positivity and brought a lot of joy to people's otherwise distraught demeanors.

As Thanksgiving approached and we were all still practically living at the hospital—David's parents literally so—I knew that I had to bring some normalcy to this situation we found ourselves in. My heart ached for Dr. and Mrs. Raborn, and I wanted them to have some sort of a Thanksgiving, because after all, we all had the fact that David was still alive to be thankful for and that was worth celebrating! So I planned a potluck Thanksgiving dinner with about 25 of our friends, where the plan was to surprise the Raborns with a feast at the hospital.

I took care of the logistics and prepared the main courses and had everyone bring a side to share. We all arrived at the hospital, food in hand, to a very grateful and emotional Dr. and Mrs. Raborn. We sat around a huge long table and shared a prayer as well as what each one of us was grateful for that Thanksgiving. It was a wonderful evening that brought people together in joy and lifted spirits, even though ultimately it was all because of grim circumstances. It proved to me that beauty can be found anywhere, and in any circumstance.

16. UNSTOPPABLE
Veronica Jubinville

If I had to choose one word to describe David, it would be this: unstoppable.

I've known David since junior high school, which is going back about 15 years now. He was a popular guy, known for his great sense of humour and his talents on both the basketball court and football field. He often walked through the halls of Bev Facey High School high-fiving friends and teachers with a big grin on his face.

Fast-forward several years to his accident, and I remember exactly where I was when I heard the news. I was a young journalist working at CTV Saskatoon, and was sitting in the newsroom when I got the call.

I remember my friend on the other end of the line telling me that David had had an accident on his bike. She said he had gone over the handlebars headfirst into the pavement and had been taken to the nearest hospital. When I learned he had had to undergo emergency surgery because the swelling in his brain was so severe, it was hard to hold back the tears.

It's fair to say my reaction was a mix of sadness, shock, and a feeling of helplessness. I was comforted knowing that many of David's friends and family had made their way to the hospital to be by his side.

I was able to travel home not long after the accident to visit David and remember a wave of sadness and grief after seeing him for the first time. It was hard to see someone who was so full of life lying in a hospital bed with contusions, bruises, and tubes everywhere.

As the months continued, I tried to visit as much as I could, but it was difficult living 500 kilometres away. I, and many others, would follow the updates from the Facebook page that Adam Tuckwood created, and send David messages of hope and positivity for a full recovery.

By the time you're reading this part of the book, you probably know the whole story. However, I feel it's important to emphasize: the fact that David made a full recovery after five months in a coma and three months of rehabilitation is nothing short of a miracle.

During David's recovery, I had made the move to CTV Edmonton, working as a reporter. I approached him to ask if he wanted to share his story, and when he said yes, I was thrilled.

As a journalist, you're always searching for stories to tell — stories that are unique, relatable, different, engaging, inspiring, and informative. It's true that newscasts are often full of tragedies, crime, and stories about struggle. But there are also stories of hope, of communities coming together, and of positive programs that make a real difference in people's lives.

For me, David's story was so much more than his remarkable road to recovery. His story and message was one of strength, perseverance, and resiliency in the face of adversity.

David not only had to learn to walk again, but he also had to learn to talk and eat again. He tested his patience when he had to learn how to use every muscle and bone in his body to ensure his mobility would return back to normal. The thought of even doing that — never mind actually doing it — is absolutely impossible to most people. I can only imagine how painful, tiring, stressful, and overwhelming his rehabilitation must have been.

As I was gathering interviews for the story, I interviewed the man who found him on the road, his neurosurgeon, his parents, a friend, and his doctor at the Glenrose Rehabilitation Hospital. Although each one of these people had a different perspective on the story, one thing remained the same: if anyone was going to do this, it was David.
One of the most important parts of the story that aired on CTV Edmonton, or perhaps the one that struck a chord with people who watched it, was the part about David updating his Facebook status. After several months of being in a coma

and offline (obviously), the first update David wrote with his own two hands was, "Hey guys, did I miss anything?"

I remember my news director laughing when he read this part of the story. I also remember many people telling me it was their favourite part of the story. These six words alone are a perfect example of David's sense of humour and positive outlook during what was surely the toughest fight of his life.

I wanted to tell David's story, not only for him, his family and friends, but mostly for the viewers who have been in similar accidents or scenarios. I wanted people to know that wearing a helmet saved his life. I wanted people to know that even when you're enduring the most difficult journey you've ever encountered, that it is possible to do so with grace and dignity. I wanted people to know that his doctors and therapists called his progress miraculous. David is a living and breathing example of what some people believed was impossible.

I'm not a journalist anymore, but if I were, I would continue to seek out stories like his. I think we could all use more stories of hope, healing, and success. We could all use more stories that make us stop and realize how lucky we are to be healthy and capable of doing things like going for a run and eating a meal without assistance.

I know David is grateful to be here today. I know he is dedicated to raising money and giving back to the facilities that gave him so much. And I know he will continue to impress and surprise us with whatever is yet to come.

I am proud to call David my friend, and if you're reading this, it means his courageous story has somehow touched your life, too.

Today, I would still use one word to describe David, and that word is...

Unstoppable..

17. AN ANGEL IN HOSPITAL
Diane Raborn

Day after grueling day, our son lay in a coma having suffered a traumatic brain injury with only the use of machines to keep him alive and here with us. His body was bloated; his eyes black, sunken, and closed; and his head bandaged, yet exposing the open gorge where almost half of his skull had been removed. Sporadically, his electrolytes lost balance and his heart rate zoomed to dangerous levels as the rest of his vital signs were monitored minute by minute while we held our breath in the hospital's Neurological Intensive Care Unit.

It was the beginning of fall.

This was too difficult for any parent to internalize with impossible choices thrown at his father and me in our vulnerable state. During the course of these first few traumatic days, we knew that our state of confusion and inner chaos could easily envelop our thoughts and emotions. As a consequence, our actions and behaviour could result in skewed perceptions with poor decision-making abilities as a possible outcome. We both needed to immediately come to terms with the enormity and scope of the situation at hand. Looming questions pierced our hearts. Arrows of despair bowed our heads.

Our hearts quickly discerned the importance of joining together in faith with our Lord God of hope, mercy, and love. My husband and I both knew without a shimmer of a doubt that we needed His guidance now more than ever. We humbly joined our minds toward listening to Jesus, hearing the Lord of our life in a very real way, as we stayed positive in His Light. And we understood that this meant giving all of our problems and burdens over to Him in a truly committed sense. Not just some, not the bulk, but the *entirety* of every care and concern. The gloom in our hearts was radically dissipated as the weight from our shoulders disappeared. While the potential of building a wall of stone around our hearts existed at any given time, prevention and love came in the very Name of Jesus Christ. In embracing Him, our hope grew.

The choice was ours and we chose to lean on the divinity of the Trinity. Each day we saw blessings in many forms. What better time to reach out to others as we accepted and gave blessings. Instead of doubt, we chose faith. Instead of fear, we chose hope. Instead of remorse, hate, bitterness, or destructive thoughts, we chose prayer. All conscious, focused avenues. All within our grasp.

Yes, at times we slipped and slid into the depth of darkness. But it was always the wrong path. How could we help our family if we waded into the waters of sludge? Negativity always means loss. When one or the other of us fell into its grip, the positive pull of grace would push us upward. Positivity always brings gain to the forefront. And working in the positive position of light allows determination, reality, firmness, goodness, and graciousness to co-exist toward a healthy goal. Our goal was to stay the course in the Light for our son's full recovery.

The road was rocky and storms prevailed. Every day the path was laden with barricades. Daily, an angel came to stay and help to lift the barriers that had presented themselves overnight. Her name is Janet, and she shall always be remembered for the angel that she is in her truly benevolent, warm, and intelligent manner. Each day she helped us to move forward as she graciously aided our son. Having previously worked as an ICU nurse, her expertise was invaluable and appreciated. She brought love, hope, and friendship. *As only an angel can do.*

The many friends who visited were extraordinary. They selflessly brought their time and energy along with kindness, joy, love, and support. Angels *'in hospital.'* Continuously and tirelessly they came and helped to sustain us through the trials of multiple surgeries, pneumonias, infections, hospital gowns in isolation, and long periods of waiting. *Angels acting as angels.* Grateful, we will always remember them in our hearts. Forever.

Julian Marchand was instrumental in bringing a consistent sense of encouragement and energy. He never failed to bring calmness and common sense as he approached a variety of situations. These situations were uniquely medical, and often

101

in crisis mode. Julian was a huge help to us and continually lifted our spirits. He reassured me when I need it the most. For his time, energy, and helpfulness I am very grateful. *Thank you, Julian!*

An Angel Pastor. Rita Penner brought wonderful friendship and spiritual consolation. Her strength, her voice of clarity, and her guidance gave much comfort during this dark period when a battle seemed to wage at every turn. Rita, a pastor, always had the right words, especially when we all felt voiceless. What I needed to hear were those words I could hold up to the Light to keep me strong. And she always knew those words. She used the fighting words of passages of Scripture to lift me up. I used them daily and kept them in my heart. *Thank you, Rita.*

Angels on the home front brought food, stayed with my 87-year-old mom, and made our life outside the hospital continue to work. And their timing was always perfect! These angels provided sustenance, comfort, and grace and will never be forgotten. One even put in a much-needed downstairs bathroom for mom. Our renovation began before Dave's accident. Later, it became necessary to change our laundry room into a new bathroom across the hall from our large main floor den, which would become mom's new bedroom, bringing her down from upstairs. John Mol, who'd previously helped put in a back deck and renovate our outdated kitchen, was ever-present at home during those long hours in the hospital. It was a great solace knowing mom was not alone but with a family friend. And our home renovation went off without a hitch. I can honestly say that I didn't give it a moment's thought. *Thank you, angels on the home front*!

Family came as angels. *An angel for a brother* who provided all that he had, every ounce of his being and every precious gift he could bestow. Through this brother's inspiration, Taylor inspired us all with his wonderfully written updates. With love, he stayed beside his brother, held his hand, and breathed words of encouragement in a bond that had always existed and was as strong as silver. With love he prayed, instinctively engaged, and offered practical and unique ideas toward recovery. An angel with the bond of gold.

An Angel of an Aunt came. A doctor with varied experiences, she came several times to offer her medical support and love. An angel who brought firsthand years of knowledge and one who prayed with us and over our son. She offered the priceless time and energy of a generous angel. An amazing angel!

Another Angel Aunt, this one an expert in speech and language facilitation, gave us blessings resulting in a breakthrough of this essential area in a TBI. Her cheerfulness, love, and positive outlook always led to smiles, and we treasured her visits. An angel who smoothed the way to recovery. An awesome angel!

An Angel Sis came and read to our son. She was a calm, devoted, and treasured angel throughout the worst of times. She was steady and strong, and she sat at length with her brother in a small, shared hospital room. An angel to be cherished.

However, it was near the end of October in the large isolation room in the ICU ward when the angel who will always remain with me appeared. An unexpected apparition. Up to this point I had barely left the hospital. When Dave was struggling with erratic vitals, the inflammation of infection, and a newly discovered deep vein thrombosis, I was determined to stay overnight once again on a very familiar library chair—the one in the corner that would collapse on command. My husband left the ICU room at 9:30 PM. As on every other night, he would bring the car around to the front of the hospital and wait for me. If I didn't show up by 11:00 PM, he'd return home. This was something he'd done since the beginning of our hospital trial. I told him yet again that tonight I could not leave.

Wearing the mandatory yellow robe, gloves, and mask, I pulled down the shades, turned off the lights, and tuned in the medically recommended CD, "*Bach for the Brain.*" I moved a plastic chair close to the hospital bed. Each breath was measured with the inserted tube and hospital infection. Tonight I hoped for a sweet sleep for our son, unlike the restless ones of late. Then I opened up my Bible to the centre to read some soothing psalms. I found myself in the lamenting Psalm 77, which somehow spoke to me. Twice, I read it. My heart flinched.

It was then that I turned to the 23rd Psalm to find solace. My eyes looked up and I saw it. As if from another dimension, a demarcation over our son's heart opened up and I watched, stunned, as an angel exited in breathtaking gloss and glimmer. Dave's vital signs had been very volatile during so much of the first month; however, those were nothing compared to this night. "*His heart might not make it tonight*", the nurse had said to me. "*It's his heart rate. It's beating extraordinarily fast.*" Not that I'd left yet at this point. Or would I have left. The angel was silver, gold, with colours in all brilliance. It was small, fast, and enthralling. How long was it there? For a second or an hour? I was riveted by the glimpse of this glorious sight hovering over my son's chest. Relief flooded my senses as I glanced at the large wall clock.

It was 10:31 PM.

I raced out of the hospital to find my husband waiting in the car in the cold of a northern fall night; he was overjoyed to bring me home. By its mere presence, an angel assured me that our son would make it through the night and my heart sang. *Hallelujah!*

It wasn't until much later that the significance of the time came to light. Our oldest son, Taylor, was born at 10:31 PM.

18. HOKIES?
Diane Raborn

I'd not met the basketball player I'd heard about from David over the years before David's sudden and life-changing cycling accident. But I knew his name and that his brother had received a scholarship from "The Spiders" in Richmond, Virginia. When I was introduced to Jamaal Bucknor outside the ICU on the fourth floor of the University of Alberta Hospital, I knew exactly who I was meeting. I knew that this was a basketball powerhouse. It was necessary to look up and then look up some more as I gave this gentle, kind man a hug. His power reverberated throughout my body. Immediately I sensed a man who was a true 'light.'

Calling on the phone outside the ICU to enter, we were given the yellow robes, masks, and gloves to enter the isolation room. Dave was always in isolation, it seemed. Watching the nurses return to search for a larger yellow robe for Jamaal lightened the fog of gloom. Even I chuckled when I saw the robe barely close, the sleeves end at his elbows and the hem at his mid-thigh. I cannot remember if the protocol required a hair bonnet for the long, thick dreadlocks on this formidable basketball player. Some things are just a blur. However, there are many things that are crystal-clear, things that seem to appear as if on a current screen in my mind. Jamaal came often. Since it was always the scene of nurses searching for larger sizes of yellow robes, I'm sure I can accurately state that David was in isolation, whether in ICU or on the neurology ward. Laughter *always* surrounded Jamaal's visits.

On one such visit, I asked David about Jamaal's brother at the University of Richmond, who was with "The Spiders." David knew the team name. Then I started quizzing him on other NCAA school nicknames. This is a project with a whiteboard I started with Dave in the ICU to prove to the nurses that "there was something in there." One side of the board had ten NCAA schools while the other side reflected the team names of these schools in no particular order. Vertically positioned on the left side were the following schools: UNC, University of South Carolina, Florida, Georgia, Tennessee, Iowa, Indiana, LSU, Alabama, and Purdue. Then the column on the right side contained the school names scattered in a random order: Gators, Crimson Tide, Hoosiers, Tigers, Gamecocks, Tar Heels, Boilermakers, Hawkeyes, Bulldogs, and Volunteers. Then I gave David a coloured dry-erase pen adapted and wrapped with heavy tape (the tape made it easier to hold) so that he could match one column with the next. The lines may have been quite squiggly, taking what seemed forever; but, he connected them flawlessly—even Purdue, the Boilermakers! Although the ICU nurses were a bit bewildered over my ecstatic joy when I shared 'the whiteboard project', my heart leapt: "See, he's in there! I knew it!"

So now when Jamaal mentioned that he didn't know any other NCAA team nicknames, I was quick to offer to teach them to him. He was 'game' for it and we had a lot of fun going back and forth with the NCAA schools. Jamaal was, of course, a quick study. One memory that brings a Jamaal-sized ear-to-ear smile to my face took place on the fourth-floor atrium of the U of A Hospital while we were sitting on the stone wall. We were playing *Team Name Match-Up* once again. Jamaal was doing great! I ran many extra teams by him, such as Minnesota ("Golden Gophers"), Texas A&M ("Aggies"), Stanford ("Cardinals"), Michigan ("Wolverines"), Santa Clara ("Banana Slugs"), TCU (Horned Frogs), and Maryland ("Terrapins"). And then Jamaal looked at me and asked, "But what's Virginia Tech?" I simply drew a blank. David and Taylor's aunt and uncle live very close to this beautiful university in Blacksburg, Virginia. I should have known this one, but I simply could not bring it to mind.

Then Jamaal suggested, "Let's go see David and find out what he thinks." Did I mention that Jamaal is a very positive fellow? So, we walked down to the single room on the corner where Dave was, once again, in isolation. Jamaal squeezed into a large yellow robe, mask, and snug gloves with the nurses trying their best to tie it up in the back ... on their tippy-toes!

We entered his room and I said, "David, we have a problem. Jamaal doesn't know what the team name of Virginia Tech is, and neither do I. We're counting on you!" Jamaal and I both laughed.

We were in an isolation room on the neurology ward as David, my son, languished in a coma hooked up to machines with highly contagious *C. diff*, having just gotten over pneumonia and losing weight each day. Chasing despair away was a daily event. Laughing at anything was a God-given choice, and Jamaal made it an easy one.

Dave's arm was so thin and so weak that just reaching it up instinctively to scratch his nose was hard. But his eyes lit up and followed us as we walked in. It is always in the eyes, I think. And Dave's eyes were always full of light, even when his skin was grey, his face puffy, and bags reigned under his eyes. They were the eyes of a soul fighting to hold on.

I brought out the ever-present whiteboard and attached marker. "So what do you call the Virginia Tech guys?" And I wrote "Virginia Tech" on the board. Jamaal reached down past the rails to give Dave a low, easy fist-pump. It was apparent that everything that touched David hurt him, even the sheets.

I placed the pen in Dave's hand, and he scrawled a crooked blue line. And then, in tiny letters almost too hard to decipher, he wrote "*h o k i e s.*" I knew this could not be right. Maybe he meant *Huskies.* Of course, that's what he meant. But my heart sank a bit, since it showed that Dave had missed a Team Name Match-Up for the first time. I looked at Jamaal and said, "*He meant Huskies*". I even took the marker and inserted a little 's' and made the '*o' into* a '*u.'* "Hey, Dave, can you do that again? Ya know, the nickname for Virginia Tech?" I'm obsessed. And I'm worried. Again, I place the pen in Dave's hand over the adapted heavy roll of tape (an occupational therapist's trick). Yet again, David wrote, small but legible: "*h o k i e s.*" Turning to Jamaal, I said, "Well, I'm sure he meant Huskies. Oh well." I was really trying not to worry. But "hokies"?

We had tired Dave out and he shut his eyes. This was usually a sign that visiting was over, most evident during his time in isolation. Leaving the room, I heard Wayne's shoes and particular pattern of walking coming down the hospital hall. (This was highly recognizable by this time.) I recall almost running into his arms. "Dave didn't know Virginia Tech's nickname!"

"You mean the Hokies?" he asked. "He didn't know the *Hokies*?"

19. WIGGLE WIGGLE WIGGLE WIGGLE WIGGLE...YEAH!
Amanda Johnston, *MSc PT, Glenrose PT*

When I first met David, I was a newly graduated physiotherapist working at the Glenrose Rehabilitation Hospital in Edmonton. David had recently been admitted to the Inpatient Adult Brain Injury unit after a lengthy stay in acute care.

In my first session with David, he was not able to actively participate in much of the assessment due to the severity of his injury. He required a motorized ceiling lift to move from the full support wheelchair onto the treatment plinth. He was awake but didn't speak. At this point in time, David needed help with almost every activity; he was not eating, talking, or able to move on his own. His brother, clearly a positive and cheerleading influence in David's recovery so far, accompanied him to this first assessment and helped us to get to know David better. We came up with a treatment plan and started with the basics: moving his limbs through range of motion, active movements of his arms and legs, and some assisted sitting balance.

One of my earlier memories of David was during a therapy session of walking with the platform walker. This was a three-person job involving David, Tamara the rehab assistant, and me. Additionally, one of his friends (Julian Marchand) had come to support him. At this point, David was participating in therapy, would answer questions briefly, but had yet to initiate any speech or show emotion. Julian had an iPod playing "LMFAO" (workout jams) for motivation. Specifically, the song "Sexy and I Know It" was playing. As we

110

were waiting for David to regain the energy to walk another few steps, he suddenly chimed out, *"Wiggle wiggle wiggle wiggle wiggle wiggle...yeah!"* in time with the song! Tamara, Julian, and I all looked at each other, then all belly laughed! David even cracked a tiny smile, and that was the first moment I saw some of his personality start to shine through.

After that, things really started to progress, largely due to David's persistence and hard work. Soon David was able to walk unassisted, although with a very stiff gait pattern and limited balance. There were many sessions where I got to "push" David around, making sure he had the required balance to walk on his own. The day he was allowed to walk to his appointments without the dreaded "old person" walker was cause for celebration.

Now came the fun work! He put in a lot of time on the CAREN system (a hydraulic platform with a treadmill, body harness and floor-to-ceiling interactive screens) to improve his dynamic balance and coordination. We had impromptu sessions on the Glenrose lawn. David had been missing sports, was worried he would never play basketball again, and was losing interest in his sessions (because practicing walking, even on various surfaces and at different speeds, is still just walking...boring!). So one day I told him to drop and give me five burpees. His eyes almost popped out of his head. "I can't do a burpee!" he exclaimed. I told him to give it a try anyway. He dropped down clumsily into a plank position on the grass, and then awkwardly and with effort got back up to his feet and gave a quick hop. I cheered, *"You did it!"* He did four more, and then we walked back into the hospital. We ran into his father on the way back, and I believe the first thing

111

David said was, "Amanda's so mean; she's making me do BURPEES!" with a teary grin. His interest in therapy sessions was restored!

Pretty soon we were practicing basketball skills out back on the court: dribbling, passing, and foul shots. Three months after I first met David, unable to talk, walk or move on his own, he was discharged home from the inpatient program, talking, walking and practicing his basketball skills. David had a big impact on me as a new therapist. As David learned to speak, move, and function again, I was learning right alongside him. As a new physiotherapist I had many ideas and an open mind, but David really showed me what could be accomplished with persistence and hope. It was inspiring to see how he rose to every challenge and also how his family was there to support him every step of the way. Every time I work with someone who has suffered a brain injury and is worried about the outcome, I have David in the back of my mind, reminding me of what is possible.

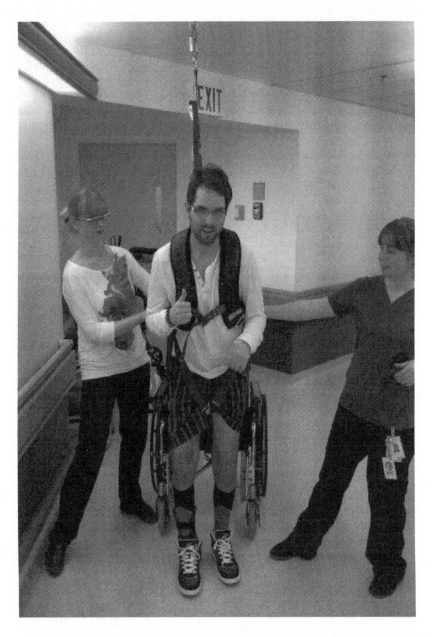

Learning to walk at the Glenrose, with PTs Amanda Johnston (left) and Tamara Auriat (right).

113

Tamara Auriat, Glenrose *PTA*

As a therapist assistant, the physiotherapist will give you a brief report of your patient prior to the initial assessment. I learned David was a young male (my age) who survived a TBI from a bicycle accident. These traumatic stories are never easy to see or hear about. When David first came down to physio, we could see the excitement he and his family had about him finally being on the path toward mobility. David was brought down to the gym of the Glenrose Rehab Hospital (GRH) in his wheelchair, and we needed to use the mechanical lift to transfer him out of his chair to the therapy bed where we began some very basic treatment with him.

One of the exercises we started with him was sitting balance, to build core stability and, ultimately, to reach one of the first goals of him being able to sit on his own with no support from others. I would sit behind David on the bed and the physiotherapist would sit in front; from there his physio journey began. In the beginning, it was very simple (in theory) and repetitive, but this exercise was a very important stepping stone toward his goals, one of them being to play basketball again. We take this very seriously in physio as it helps motivate patients to do things that they love and to work toward their own personal and passionate goals. But David didn't need any motivation; he was determined and hard-working from the beginning and throughout his sessions (despite moments of frustration).

He and his family's excitement never faded; it kept growing and changing as he continually and quickly progressed. He was a huge encouragement to other patients, always coming down to physio with a huge smile and high fives for everyone. We were always excited about his arrival. I'd be lying if I said that it wasn't a pleasure to work with David and to see his incredible progress. In fact, it was beyond a pleasure; it was by far the most memorable and impactful experience I had while working at the GRH. It was incredible to see this young man's journey go from next-to-zero mobility to (in a short 3-month period) jogging, playing tennis, shooting basketballs, jumping, and doing running crossovers. It was one of the best experiences I have ever been a part of. Tears, laughter, and pure amazement came with his short 45-minute therapy sessions. Thank you, David, for being a fundamental part of my career, but more importantly, for becoming a part of my life as someone I will never forget!

20. COURAGE, ENCOURAGED
Trina Johnson - Director, Community Relations and Fund Development at the Glenrose Rehabilitation Hospital Foundation

My first memory of David begins by hearing about him.

In early 2012, just six months into my role with the Glenrose, a board member of the Glenrose Foundation (David King) told me about a family friend who was involved in terrible freak cycling accident. He had nearly lost his life, survived a five-month coma, and was now at the Glenrose. I heard about how the parents and brother created a powerful support system to ensure someone was by his side day and night, how family and friends were openly supporting his journey through a Facebook group (*David Raborn: Updates and Prayers*), and how it was truly amazing how far he had come. He told me this because I was interested in meeting more Glenrose families to help raise funds to improve care at the hospital. To respect their privacy, he didn't give names or contact information but promised to introduce us when the time was right.

Looking back, while I heard the story, it did not stick yet. I didn't know David yet, and I certainly did not foresee what he would come to teach me.

Months later, a Dr. Raborn came to our office, introduced himself and invited a representative of the Glenrose Foundation to come up to the unit that afternoon to meet his son David, who was being discharged. With quiet pride, Dr. Raborn shared that this was a major milestone; a reporter was coming to interview David, and they would like to present a cheque to the Glenrose Foundation from David on behalf of his friends who had raised funds in a NCAA basketball pool set up by his brother. This was May 24th, 2012, the day David left the Glenrose.

Feeling nervous, I headed up to the unit. Because of my unique role of fundraising for the hospital, I did not often interact with patients and went on the units even less.

I spotted Dr. Raborn at the entrance and met David face-to-face for the first time. As I walked over, David simplified things right away with the good ol' fashioned, "Hi, my name is David. What's your name?" I felt calmer instantly. We then

116

posed for a photo, and David shared how a reporter and friend were about to do the interview. So I just tagged along, watching the interview from the sidelines and learning about his journey firsthand. Mrs. Raborn and Dr. Raborn also shared how hard they had advocated to get David to the Glenrose because they believed in him so much. I respectfully asked for permission to join the *David Raborn: Updates and Prayers* Facebook group, and that is when I really began to know David.

Having only joined Facebook in September of 2011, the benefit was not yet clear. What was all the hype? Why did people like it so much? David and his family and friends showed me how it was a platform of support. How staying connected and celebrating the milestones in life allowed us all to become stronger. In reading the posts, I saw how David was and is a living example the Glenrose Foundation's tagline of *Courage, Encouraged.*

Part of starting to know David also introduced me to his brother, Taylor, who I feel as if I know because his posts are so authentic and eloquent. One still stays with me to this day: *"David is no longer a patient, someone with a sliver of hope to whom things are done, IVs are inserted, and procedures are administered to. Today David is doing things: dreaming dreams, making plans, living his life."*

Each post celebrated their renewed passion for everything life offers.

Then I asked David for help. We were creating a video to celebrate the courage of Glenrose patients: would he be willing to be in the video? David said yes. *Phew again*! We filmed him shooting hoops in the Glenrose gym and then literally followed him walking out of the hospital to live his life.

The following April, the Raborns attended the Courage Gala, and when we asked donors to stand and pledge $1,000 to help with an initiative at the hospital, Dr. Raborn stood, giving in David's honour. He told me afterwards, "How could I not?"

Even with all of this, I still really didn't know David because our interactions had always been brief. Then one day, David sent me a Facebook message about a bike event in Ontario with the comment, "Surely there would be interest in YEG?" ("YEG" is the airport code for Edmonton.) At the same time, two board members were planning an outdoor ride around Pigeon Lake, which would become the *Courage Ride for Rehab*.

David didn't hesitate. For the first time since the accident, he would ride again. And not just around the block: 58.8 kms. In true "David-style," he graciously volunteered his time to come on the news and promote the event bright and early at 7:00 AM on a crisp Monday morning.

All I could think was, "What does it take to get on a bike again? How do you find the courage to face that fear to do once again what almost killed you? What did his parents and brother think about him riding again?" So I asked him in the green room.

David was honest. He had to convince his mom and dad, and his brother was still struggling with David's decision to ride. To him it was simple because he felt so strongly about giving back to those who had cared for him. It would confirm that he's back. That he is 100%.

On race day in September of 2016, I was a passenger in Dr. Raborn's car watching David conquer this goal. Again I felt nervous, yet Dr. Raborn was totally calm. We reminisced about life, sports, and parenthood. Once again, I got to know a little more about David and the deep respect and bond between him and his parents, not to mention his sense of humour. When we stopped to check in with David, he always had a smile, even though we didn't really tell him about the hills he literally had to climb or despite the fact that he had bought biker shorts that were too small so he was wearing basketball shorts over them. He was doing it. He met his goal. Here we are living life's rat race, tackling our 'to dos', although, most us are not internalizing the privilege of those lists and demands. David and his family faced questions most of us will never have to ask ourselves, or answer for that matter. David's journey is a lesson for us all. *Relish the journey. Celebrate. Give back.*

His enthusiasm to set big goals and always improve is the reminder all of us need to never rest on our laurels but rather to look beyond ourselves. Thank you for all this and more, David.

Handing Trina Johnson the cheque from our "March Madness fundraiser".

21. GOD'S NOT FINISHED YET
Pastor James Avery

I just don't think that God is done yet. That feeling, more of a nudge from God, was what both Pastor Matt and I felt as we walked out of the room after seeing Dave motionless and hooked up to what seemed like countless machines. It wasn't the first time that I had been to see Dave, and it certainly wasn't the last. I didn't know why, but I was sure that there had to be more to his story. "It's not time for David to be called to heaven yet" was what I kept thinking that night and for the following days, weeks, and months of his recovery.

That feeling was certainly contrary to the news that the family had been given. As I sat with Wayne and Diane, they shared that the possibility of David's survival was not good. The seconds seemed to take forever to pass as I sat with some family members and close friends in that small room. I don't remember what I said to his family, or what was spoken as we prayed together.

When I left Diane and Wayne, I was torn, shaken to my very core. On the one hand, it was easy to see the devastation and almost hopelessness of the situation. The way that they looked and the heavy burden that they endured will forever be etched in my memory. Yet on the other hand was this feeling that things would work out somehow ... a belief coming from the truth that God is alive and active and that He just wasn't finished. A belief that there was more for Dave to do on this earth.

To say that his bike accident impacted a multitude of people is an understatement. I was helping to coach my son's football team and was just finishing up practice when I received the news of the accident. The details were a little vague: something about a bike accident and Dave being rushed to the University of Alberta Hospital.

Faith and football are common bonds that Dave and I share. He was (and is) a strong and talented athlete who used his athletic gifts to share his faith and to impact people. After the accident, some friends [Adam Tuckwood] started a Facebook page and it was instantly filled with messages of support for Dave. There were T-shirts made and beards grown in hope and support. There are countless people whose lives are intersected and changed through knowing Dave.

Positive role models seem hard to come by in this day and age. That is perhaps one of the biggest reasons that my son, Nathan, was drawn to Dave. It didn't take Nathan long to notice the tattoo that Dave has on his bicep: Philippians 4:13. It's a verse that rings true. A verse that tells part of Dave's story: "*I can do all things through Christ Jesus who gives me strength.*"

When Nathan learned of Dave's accident, he started putting a piece of tape around his arm that had *Philippians 4:13* written on it before every football game that he played. It wasn't long before his entire team was wearing tape around their arms. That year, his team won the Tier 1 city finals, and the day after the championship game, Nathan brought the trophy in to the hospital for Dave to see.

It had been several weeks since the accident, and several surgeries had taken place. There had been glimmers of hope as well as setbacks along the way. The chances of Dave surviving were said to be low; the chances of him talking, and eating, and sitting up, and standing up, and walking were also said to be low. Hope was fleeting, but God wasn't finished, and He still isn't.

Dave eventually moved from the University of Alberta Hospital to the Glenrose Rehabilitation Hospital. He was like superman. It seemed that every time he was told that he would never be able to do something again, he would just push that much harder to do that very thing.
Looking now, more than five years since the accident, *it is evident to me that God is still not done.*

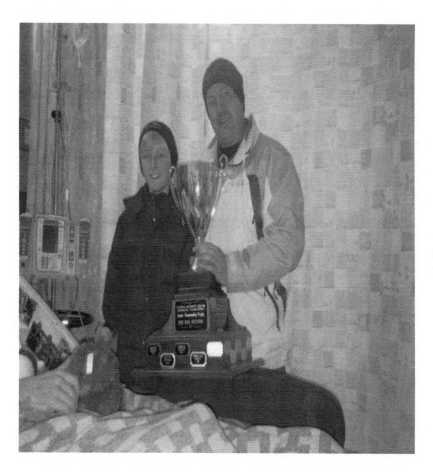

Pastor James Avery (right) with son Nathan (left) showing me the
championship trophy his team earned!

22. MY FATHER'S PERPECTIVE
Dr. Wayne Raborn

The afternoon of the 22nd of September 2011 was a beautiful early fall day in Strathcona County. The trees had begun to develop their amazing yellow and orange hues, and the farmers were busy baling hay for the winter. We live on an acreage. Fall is my favourite time of the year, especially in Virginia in the Shenandoah Valley and in the mountains of Western North Carolina. David and I had been working together on some of the usual items that are related to a home-based real estate business. He decided to take off on his bicycle, and was stopping every so often on the side of the road to take pictures with his iPhone and send them to friends via text during his fateful ride.

Earlier David and his friend had rebuilt a road bicycle that I had put together in Chapel Hill in the late '70s, before I met his mother. It was now in top shape, and David asked my assistance in selecting a proper helmet from a local bicycle shop. He settled on a model that would be appropriate for longboarding as well as bicycling.

David had a history of concussions from playing football for the University of Calgary Dinos as a wide-receiver, punt and kick-off returner. I was concerned that he use proper headgear for bicycling. In fact, I was not a big supporter of bicycling alone as a result of assessing people at various hospital emergency clinics over the years in my dental surgeon's capacity. This included the University of Alberta Hospital Dental Clinic. After David's accident, the cases came flooding back in my memory. Before Dave's accident, one of

125

our clients—a retiring dentist of my age group—was knocked from his bicycle while riding with friends in the area near Leduc, Alberta. He was struck by one of the long extended rearview mirrors that many pick-up trucks have these days (that allow them to view around and behind the trailers that they are towing). Fortunately, he was merely knocked into the ditch and received non-life-threatening injuries.

David was probably in the best physical shape of his life thanks to his dedication to a special program called "P90X", a rigorous program designed by trainer, Tony Horton. He had nearly completed the entire vigorous and demanding schedule. In discussing this aspect with the physicians, surgeons, and nurses that worked so diligently and skillfully to save David's life, it was mentioned many times that someone in less physical shape would not have been able to survive. In fact, one surgeon joked with me, saying that had I received the same traumatic injury at 72, in my physical condition, they would not have had a chance to assist with my survival. Also, paramount in my mind was David's athletic condition, courage, drive, and fighting spirit that came to bear literally hundreds of times over the next eight months of surgical procedures, severe infections, underfeeding through gastric tube, coma, and rehabilitation.

Finally, and probably most importantly, I believe that it was David's steadfast belief in God through Jesus Christ that took over the management of his recovery and guided the hands and hearts of what was to become a truly miraculous event.

My recollection, not without a knot in my stomach five plus years after the event, was that I received a phone call from a Good Samaritan who had stopped his vehicle and blocked the road so that other drivers would not run over David who was lying face down on the pavement, helmet smashed on the right side and bleeding from the right ear. David was conscious enough to give Bob Lloyd and his son Robbie my cell number. Bob and Robbie, who were enroute to a hockey tryout in Fort Saskatchewan, were the good Samaritans who intervened and made all the difference. Bob told me later that he'd called 911. An ambulance was literally minutes away returning from Fort Saskatchewan, on the very same road. He reported that the dispatcher noted that STARS Air Ambulance would not be available faster than the emergency medical technician team, which was literally less than 15 km away.

David told Bob that a vehicle had not hit him but that his front wheel had come off the bicycle after he evidently hit a pothole on this country road while traveling south just over the crest of a small hill. The front fork of the bike dug into the black top and catapulted David onto his head before he could put his hands out to break the fall. David later felt that he was probably traveling at 25 to 30 km per hour when he encountered the pothole. When I examined the crash site a couple of days later, I note the marks of the bicycle fork and that the pothole was not a round one but a vertical crack running parallel to David's route. That would account for the wheel being dislodged.

My wife Diane and I immediately leapt into our car and raced off to the accident site, which was approximately eight miles from our home in Strathcona County. Upon arrival, we discovered that Bob and Robbie had left the scene just moments before. I did not meet them until later. Diane and I were relieved (for an instant) to see that the ambulance had arrived and that the Emergency Medical Technicians were finishing putting David into a stretcher—not without some pushback from him as he was confused and frightened.

When I first saw my son's face, my heart sank as both of his eyelids were already dark blue, the lids swollen by hematomas, and there was evidence of blood on the pavement and of course on Dave's face. I've spent a lifetime as a dental surgeon attending patients in hospital emergency facilities, including time with the U.S. Navy as part of a trauma unit in Vietnam waters. I instantly had a knot in my stomach and fear in my heart for David's recovery while the EMTs were loading David into the ambulance.

A day or so later in the University of Alberta Hospital, Diane and I thanked Bob and Robbie for their absolutely wonderful actions of blocking traffic and rerouting vehicles around our helpless son. They told me that there had been more that 25 vehicles that had dodged around the accident site and only one lady cared enough to slow down and ask if she could assist. Fortune had certainly smiled on David, as Bob and Robbie were the right people to help in the nick of time. We judged that Dave had only been on his face at the right side of the road facing south for a very few minutes before they spotted him and pulled their truck across the lane to block oncoming traffic, shielding him from further harm. Bob was able to converse with David before he became delirious, obtaining my phone number, calling 911, and comforting Dave while awaiting the ambulance.

Diane traveled with Dave in the ambulance and tried her best to comfort him and keep him from losing consciousness by asking questions, such as "where did your father play football; where did your mom go to University; where is Taylor studying and what girl did you last take out on a date?" She sang "Rocky Top" and other 'fight' songs hoping he'd chime in. I followed the ambulance. Upon arrival at the Grey Nun's Hospital after an approximate 15-minute ride, I joined Diane and David and the EMT team in the emergency triage area. I was careful not to convey my inner misgivings regarding the seriousness of David's injuries.

We found out later that the dispatcher had ascertained that the Grey Nuns was the closest hospital and that they had diagnostic radiography equipment that would allow the physicians to make some diagnostic images and ascertain where David was to be subsequently transported. The ambulance did not speed along much to our wishes but traveled at a pace that allowed the EMTs to start an IV and talk with the Grey Nuns emergency staff to advise them of the obvious extent of David's injuries.

Once we arrived at the Grey Nun's emergency facility, the EMTs immediately disembarked and were able to bring David's dire situation to the attention of the emergency physicians and nurses who made a bed available within a very short time. Then the fight began to get David's cooperation as he was struggling and pushing back and did not recognize that the people surrounding him were fighting for his life and not attacking him personally. Eventually, they had to deliver medication intravenously that relaxed Dave to the extent that they were able to get him disrobed and ready for the CT scans that were being prepared for immediately. An endotracheal tube was placed as the staff was aware of the imminent danger of David being unable to breath due to possible airway blockage. The greatest fear was that the subdural hematoma and multiple intracranial bleeds would cause severe pressure on the brain and possible death before a surgical intervention could be performed.

While this was going on, our dear friends and neighbours, Lorne and Rita Penner, arrived for moral support and constant prayers. They became our transportation for the evening as I had left our car at the Grey Nuns and we were in no condition to drive safely at this point.

The emergency room physician reported that the CT scans revealed massive skull and facial fractures on David's right side and that emergency neurosurgery was being planned at the University of Alberta Hospital. To me that was of some comfort, for I knew after being on dental staff, off and on for the past 30-plus years, that his neurosurgical service was a top-flight unit.

Little did we know at the time that the neurosurgeon on call, Dr. Michael Chow, was able to view the CT scans on his equipment at his home, and before he had even departed for the hospital, his team of surgeons, surgical nurses, and anesthesiologists were already beginning to assemble and prepare the way for David's expected arrival.

This time the ambulance was proceeding at "code three" speed with flashing lights and siren to the university hospital. We were told later that David experienced a crisis in the ambulance while being transported that required the pace to slow a bit enroute. Thankfully, the EMTs were able to manage the problem. Since we had departed via Lorne's SUV in anticipation of David's transportation via ambulance, we actually heard the ambulance arriving as were parking at the University of Alberta Hospital.

However, when we enquired at emergency services as to the condition of our son and where he was, no one had any answers. The reason for this mystery, which lasted for about an hour, was that the surgical team had met David at the emergency triage area. He was immediately and directly transported to the neurosurgical suite and was not actually admitted to the hospital until later in the process.

In reality, this was a perfectly expedient move. As we were told by Dr. Chow later, it was approximately 15 minutes after David was rolled through the emergency entrance and onto the elevator that they were "cutting skin" as part of the neurosurgical procedure. This would result in a large piece of Dave's right anterior skull (beginning just posterior to his right eye and finishing about midpoint of his ear) to be removed, along with many bone spicules created by the bone-crushing fall to the pavement via the catapulted action of his fall over the front of his bicycle.

Thank goodness again for the impact-absorbing effect of this helmet. The pressure from the large developing subdural hematoma was thus relieved (temporarily). Later that

131

eventful evening and early the next morning, the surgical team determined that more of his skull needed to be removed to allow for further expansion of his brain. Early on the morning of September 23rd, David underwent his second neurosurgical procedure and a large piece of skull was removed adjacent and posterior to the earlier surgery. My estimate is that between the two pieces removed, approximately 20% of his skull was extracted and kept in storage for their eventual and planned replacement.

Remembering the events of this life-changing accident more than five years later evokes several absolutely stunning responses by David's friends and our family, our friends, and what was to become an incredible support group. One aspect, the use of online communication programs, stunned me. I had not paid much attention to those (Facebook as an example) before David's catastrophic accident. However, because of social media and people calling and texting each other, there was a physical gathering of close friends overnight in the waiting area adjacent to the neurology ICU. For example, Julian Marchand, the starting quarterback for the Alberta Golden Bears and David's close friend, sat up all night with Diane and me. He did this despite the fact that he was facing a major football game in 48 hours. Lorne and Rita were with us as well. Over the upcoming weekend, literally dozens of David's friends from high school and the University of Calgary descended upon the ICU waiting area. Instead of the usual one or two visitors being allowed to go in to see David at a time, the staff modified the rules and groups of four to six visitors were allowed into the ICU at a time.

One poignant moment I remember well was when so many of his friends surrounded me as I explained that David's survival would not have been possible had things not gone smoothly in the rescue efforts: beginning with Bob and Robbie and moving onto the ambulance that happened to be in the area returning from another task, the Grey Nuns diagnostic services, the transport to the University of Alberta Hospital (UAH) at "code three" speed, and the well-coordinated surgical team led by Dr. Chow that was awaiting David's arrival. As I described to that crowd of folks, including many from athletic backgrounds, *"the play was drawn up and executed perfectly or David would have surely perished."* Had the accident happened further from Edmonton, even an air ambulance evacuation would have been too slow to deliver Dave in time for the surgical intervention to stop the brain swelling.

I could see the hand of God coordinating these efforts to such an extent that over the weekend, we gathered in a circle with hands on shoulders of those adjacent and recited the Lord's Prayer. Believers and non-believers came to that recognition at that amazing revelation. God had a plan for David that was not to end on that beautiful fall Thursday afternoon in the Alberta countryside.

Looking back on the group visits of that eventful first weekend, at least two of Dave's friends who upon seeing him in the ICU were so overcome by the horrible visuals that these two strong young men actually fainted. One was a football teammate of his at the U of C. Others were sickened and emerged from their brief visit visibly shaken. This has now become one of the lighter aspects recalled as people remember that fateful weekend. Some kidding among that special group has definitely occurred.

As for my involvement, I was slated to teach a seminar of dental students at 08:00 on the 23rd, and since I couldn't be of assistance awaiting David's second neurological event, I went ahead and taught the 08:00 class; in my closing remarks, I mentioned his horrific accident. This evidently ignited a ton of support among our dental students. Subsequently, my teaching continued throughout David's stay at the UAH. It was a blessing for me to continue, as a touch of stability in my life that had been shattered by this accident. In fact, during the entire time of David's hospitalization at the UAH, I only had to arrange for coverage once for a lecture. In all honesty, I really looked forward to meeting with the small groups of dental students in their problem-based small group seminars. Focusing together on each problem-based case was a welcome relief. It was great to get my mind off David and his struggles, at least for an hour or two of normality.

As the word spread, David's brother and his best friend since his birth, Taylor, flew in from Iowa City where he was completing a PhD. His support during the entire process was legendary, as was that of his future bride and fellow scientist, Linh Bui. One of the most amazing aspects was when I watched Dave's friends form a group selling "*Beards for Broborn*" T-shirts to raise money for the neurology ward at the University of Alberta. *Broborn* was a nickname given to David when he played football at the U of C (Bro = **Bro**ther, born = Ra**born**). One of the major contributors to that effort was the dental class of 2012 and other dental students whom

I was privileged to be teaching through the small group seminar series during Dave's time at the UAH.

For Diane and I, the things that kept us together and focused were our constant prayers and the support from friends and colleagues from the outset of this horrific experience. I promised that if the Almighty would let David live, I would dedicate my life to ensuring that Dave had the support and follow-up needed to make a complete recovery.

There were numerous challenges along the way, as the coma, measured by the Glascow Coma Scale, did not diminish until shortly before David's transfer to the Glenrose Rehabilitation Hospital on the 21st of February, 2012, the day after his 26th birthday.

There were at least two or three episodes brought about by the failure of antibiotics that caused David to have to be placed into isolation. Throughout this difficult time, Adam Tuckwood, Dave's former high school football and basketball teammate, who was at the time working in the UAH as a registered nurse in the kidney dialysis unit, was our "in-house" link.

The most challenging and scary of the misadventures throughout the five months in the UAH came when David's skull was replaced in late November. This is major surgery; the surgeons were very careful and more than 100 stitches were used to close the wound caused by reinsertion of the two pieces of skull, which had been saved and carefully stored after those two successful surgeries in September.

The surgery went well, and the surgery team was delighted with the results. However, some very unfortunate nursing care decisions were made the evening after the surgery. An IV infusion of an anticlotting drug too soon after the surgery caused his brain to swell, which started bleeding in the brain area, which the ward nurses did not detect. This complication was compounded by the fact it was a weekend and that the nurses did not ask for surgical assistance.

As a result, that operation had to be totally redone as an emergency procedure to save David's life once again. The most disheartening aspect was that this totally reset the recovery that he had managed, and we were back again to trying to assist with communicating by the use of a whiteboard. In fact, the physiotherapy professionals in the ward did not think Dave would ever talk or read again. They were thankfully proven wrong by the intervention of his aunt, Dr. Caroline Musselwhite, a world-class speech therapist from Arizona who continually guided our efforts to restore speech and cognition. David's mother was also an absolutely vital force in the entire rehabilitation process, and without her staying by David's bedside and sleeping in a chair or nearby couch for most of the first five months, things would have gone terribly wrong.

On a particularly drab Sunday evening, I remember wheeling David in his chair from the fourth floor neurology ward along the corridor to "The Healing Garden," the beautiful, well-cultivated garden setting of the Mazankowski Heart Institute. It was about a seven or eight-minute trip, but the place was a soothing respite from the awful feelings elicited by the suffering on the neurology ward. We were met there

136

by our dear friend, Janet Mador, as well as our pastor, Marv Ziprick from Bethel Lutheran Church, who was kind enough to dispense communion and say heartfelt prayers for David's recovery. As I watched from my seat on a bench close to David, his mother, and the pastor, I was struck by the resemblance to the Last Rites that were dispensed to our dying soldiers long ago during my time as part of a surgical unit in the Vietnam War. My heart nearly burst, but I didn't tell anyone or mention the similarity until now.

As an example, when Dave was hospitalized after the surgery as a 188-pound athlete, we watched over the first three months as he was fed via IV and a gastric tube; to our dismay, David was losing weight to the extent that in December of 2011, he was down to just under 130 pounds. After being rebuffed several times in trying to get some more fluids to our son, Diane was able to get a nurse to give some extra fluids on occasion, but that still was not helping. Finally, Diane was able to sit down with the nutritionist who was in charge of the neurology ward. She was a very kind and helpful person who sat down with Diane and David's chart and started going back page by page until they finally returned to the night he was admitted after the neurosurgery. Evidently, there had been a mistake in converting our son's weight in pounds to kilograms and back to pounds again, and the hospital had been feeding David like he was a 135-pound man not a 188-pound athlete. *Oh my goodness*! He had been starved for three months! Since he was fed only by G-tube and was in a coma, we had watched our athletic young son wither away with the repeated bouts of C-diff infections, the deep vein thrombosis (DVT), and four neurosurgical procedures while he was being fed as if he was more than 50 pounds lighter—*all because of a mistake made at admission.*

The DVT in his left leg, which occurred in the neurology ICU, complicated things immensely as the nurses had trouble remembering which leg the compression stocking was to be placed on; this resulted in the necessity of labeling each leg via felt tip pin as to which was the correct leg with the DVT. Later in the fall, as we were nearing the Christmas holidays, a venous filter was placed in Dave's inferior vena cava to attempt to block clots from reaching his upper circulatory system. The removal of this filter was a very difficult procedure, and the initial attempt at removal failed. Thankfully, another interventional radiologist attempted the removal after the first failure. (Leaving these filters in place is not conducive of long life as they are notorious for clogging and causing problems.) Again, we were blessed by the expertise of the university staff and by God's grace!

After the filter was removed, David began to improve, especially due to the increased feeding via G-tube. He still could not walk, feed himself, or speak more than a few words, but his indomitable spirit took over and he persisted. He would not quit trying to improve, and we were doing our best with the solid backing of relatives, family friends, and especially David's cadre of friends from high school and university.

The next huge hurdle was trying to get David admitted to a rehabilitation facility. There were two possibilities: one in Ponoka (the Halvar Jonson Centre) and the Glenrose Rehabilitation Centre in Edmonton. Diane and I were working hard to have the admission be at the Glenrose because of its stellar reputation but also because of its proximity. We were advised by the physiotherapists who were looking after David at the UAH that he did not fit the profile for the Glenrose. He wasn't advanced far enough, and they didn't feel he would ever improve. The speech pathologist also was very discouraging regarding his prognosis.

We are ever-grateful to this day that David's Aunt Caroline, the world-renowned speech pathologist from the U.S., advised us that David would respond if we worked with him every day. I remember reading the *Edmonton Journal* to him every morning, and I felt that he did understand what I was reading. The day that he pointed out the blue Ford F-150 in the coloured ads in response to my questioning was a huge milestone! In addition, his mom worked tirelessly with David and a whiteboard with various sports-related matching games. David knew the answers (pointing and drawing lines on the whiteboard to answer matching questions) even when visiting friends did not have a clue. We were encouraged, and our mood had to remain positive to ensure that David would get an opportunity to be transferred to the Glenrose and begin the serious tasks that lay ahead.

Spots were few and difficult to find at the Glenrose, but through the leadership shown by his mother, strategic calls and letters, and the assessment of a newly hired physical medicine specialist, the opportunity arose at the Glenrose. A day after his 26th birthday, David was transferred by ambulance to a beautiful single room at the Glenrose. He still could not talk, feed himself, or walk.

David knew his life was saved by the U of A neurosurgical expertise of Dr. Chow and his associates and by the dedicated staff that, despite the serious mishaps on the ward, had given him a chance to survive. Later, after his discharge from the Glenrose, he and his friends (led by Kevin Meleskie and Stef Williams) were able to deliver a $5,000 gift that ended up going to the physiotherapy ward from funds received from the sale of T-shirts as well as the generous donations by dental student classes of 2012 and other students and family friends.

23. MY STORY
David Raborn

By now you have (hopefully) read about my accident and subsequent recovery through the eyes of people who witnessed it first-hand. These are just a few of the many stories that happened over my eight-month stay at the University of Alberta Hospital (five months of that in a coma) and my three months at the Glenrose Rehab Hospital. I'll now give you the rundown from my point of view.

This story begins as I was starting to turn a corner in my life and beginning to see some promise in my future. I was working with two amazing and creative people, Shaun Brandt and Cam Service, to develop a tech start-up that I had dreamed up a few months prior. Things were progressing to the point where we had a working mobile prototype as well as a functioning webpage. The company was called "Giraffe" and its purpose was to assist people in finding someone of the opposite sex to join them in various activities and events that were of interest to both parties. I was planning on using money from the job as an associate that I had recently accepted at ROI Corporation, the best firm in Canada that sells and appraises healthcare practices. I was happy with life, having just attended a good friend's amazing wedding in Ontario before driving down to New York City to visit another very good friend (Taylor Fuchs) where we had an amazing time, enjoying a myriad of sporting events!

In a word, things were exciting. I was in the best shape of my life, having just finished the intense home gym workout program, P90X. I felt nothing could stop me.

Maybe not, but something could sure postpone things for a while.

That something happened on a beautiful Thursday evening on September 22nd, 2011. I was out for a bicycle ride, something I was really into that summer. It was a beautiful day, so for me there was nothing better to do than ride before the sun went down. I was riding through rural Alberta, east of Sherwood Park and Edmonton, stopping every so often to take photos of what I thought were beautiful landscapes and sending them to my brother and other friends. The bike I was riding was my dad's old road bike from the '70s that I'd fixed up. It was in pretty good shape, and I was certainly proud of it. My helmet was on, and when I pedaled, I liked to go fast!

When Bob and Robbie Lloyd found me on the pavement, I was just over the crest of a hill on Range Road 223. My front wheel was off the bike and I was lying next to it, conscious.

141

They think I hit a pothole that jarred the wheel from the bike. I was astonishingly able to tell these amazing Good Samaritans that I fell from my bike and to give them my father's cell number. They called 911, and the ambulance dispatchers began trying to find an ambulance to come pick me up. They were at first looking at sending a STARS helicopter but quickly realized that an ambulance was on that very same road heading back from a call in Fort Saskatchewan. (That's some good timing if you ask me!) The paramedics were there in a couple of minutes and started working on me. The closest hospital was the Grey Nuns Hospital in Mill Woods (a subdivision in Edmonton), so they took me there, where they did a few tests, x-Rays, and a CT scan. The CT scan was sent to Dr. Michael Chow, a prominent neurosurgeon in Edmonton. He saw these pictures on his laptop at home, gathered his team together and met me at the University of Alberta Hospital. I wasn't even admitted at the hospital, as they took me right up to the surgical suite. They proceeded to take pieces of fractured bones out of my head, as well as remove a big chunk (about a fourth) of my skull from my head as my brain was swelling far too fast. They took even more of my skull out the next day. For a couple of months in the hospital, I was chillin' in my hospital bed with only gauze to prevent my brains from hanging out. For five months, I rotated from ICU to the operating table, to different floors and units, but I was always in a hospital bed. For most of my stay at the U of A Hospital, I was in Units 4A and 4B, the hospital's neurology wards.

One of the main questions I get asked about being in a coma is, "What do you remember about those five months?" The answer to that question is fairly complex. However, the definition of a coma is when "one doesn't create any new memories during that time period." The whole experience was wild for my friends and family who visited during visiting hours and expected to see me sleeping the time away, not able to respond. I had also lost the ability to talk due to the massive trauma that was inflicted on my brain. My brain had to be rewired to be able to talk, walk, swallow, and do many other basic tasks, as I had lost many fundamental functions following the trauma to my head. So, to supplement the loss of my ability to speak, my dear mother had me use a whiteboard to answer questions. Through this whiteboard, I was able to communicate with my friends and family. Picture this: my eyes are open, and I'm answering questions and looking directly at you; I've even been told that I could smile, although that happened very rarely. It would seem as if I'm "all there," right? Well, not really. I don't have any recollection of any of these encounters, except for one with my older brother, Taylor, and his girlfriend (now wife), Linh.

I had never met Linh in person since they were both doing their PhDs in biology (genetic biology — crazy smart, I know) far away, at the University of Iowa. Linh is from a suburb of Saigon, Vietnam, pretty much the middle of the jungle. And she came up to visit me during their Christmas break. So Linh is visiting me in the hospital, and she notices that there are quite a few Vietnamese nurses taking care of me. Then she teaches me a phrase that I could use when I found my voice, to tell the nurses to leave me alone. She taught me to tell my nurses to "di ra" meaning, "go out." For some reason, this is my only true memory of being in the coma. I believe I remember this because everything about it was so new. Linh was new to me, and I had never heard a Vietnamese word in

143

my life. So, for me, this memory is precious for a couple of reasons; first, it's my only memory of the U of A Hospital, and second, it's my first memory of my sister-in-law.

Coming out of a coma is not what everyone makes it out to be. I didn't all of a sudden open my eyes and walk out of the room. It was a gradual process. Once the patient has passed the Glasgow Coma Scale, they are deemed to be "out of the coma." This neurological scale is the method that records the conscious state of a patient. Patients are initially assessed and then measured later against this initial assessment. There are three elements to this scale: eye, verbal, and motor. (See the appendix for a sample chart.) The score for a completely conscious person is 15, while someone completely out of it has a score of 3, which is where I was for much of my stay at the U of A Hospital. Even once I had *passed* this test (on paper), the weeks and months following are still a groggy haze to me. I definitely remember many chunks of my stay at the Glenrose, but a lot of it is just a blur. People close to me still tell me about visits or things that I did there that are news to me.

What I do remember of the Glenrose's world-class facility was the amazing rehab that they put me through, and the staff who were truly phenomenal. I am absolutely blessed in how I was treated (at both the U of A and the Glenrose). Once I could walk and eat and talk a bit, they had me "train" on a virtual reality treadmill called the CAREN (Computer Assisted Rehabilitation Environment) located in the Courage in Motion (CIM) Centre. This machine is the first of its kind in western Canada, acquired through a partnership with the Canadian Department of National Defense, and is used for

144

both Glenrose patients and the Canadian Forces. First, they strap you in a harness like you're going to go race NASCAR. Then, they had me walking at a decent pace (or at least what qualified as a decent pace for me at the time) while a video game was going on a projection screen in front of me. That video game had a bunch of birds whizzing by me at a breakneck speed! (Ha ha! Well, maybe not, but they were zooming pretty fast for me at the time.) The more birds I could hit with my hands as they swooped past me, the more points I received. They had even made recovering from a bike accident into a fun game! The more I "played" on the CAREN, the better my balance got, and I progressed further at walking around. At first my balance was really bad and it was pretty scary for me, but after a few times on the CAREN, my physio ladies, Amanda and Tamara, took me out and I got to play tennis and even basketball! I wasn't playing like I had in the past, of course, but just being on the court got me excited!

24. ONGOING RECOVERY
David Raborn, B. Comm

Over the past years since the accident, I have had the privilege to maintain in civilian life the support that I had in the hospital. I've had the absolute honour to be able to call my amazing father my colleague and mentor. Over the years he's taught me how to be classy, to have principles, to be moral in every situation, and to always be decent. This isn't always easy when working in real estate as we do. As I said earlier, we work for ROI Corporation, Canada's professional practice appraisal and sales leader. By "professional

145

practice", I mean dental, veterinary and optometry clinics —
mostly dental, however, and that works for us well, as Dr.
Wayne Raborn is the former dean of dentistry at the
University of Alberta. ROI Corp has been amazing to me,
keeping the job for me that I had before the accident, and
providing me with annual training.

I've also been able to continue to work with kids, as my good
friend from high school, Vince Reynolds, asked me to coach
high school boys' basketball with him the fall after I got out of
the hospital, and I've been coaching the Strathcona Christian
Academy Eagles ever since.

I was able to be the best man in my brother's beautiful
wedding over Thanksgiving in October of 2015. That was
something that no one would have ever imagined I'd be able
to be a part of just a few years before. And thanks to my
Toastmasters training, I was able to nail the best-man speech
that I was really worried about!

In the winter of 2015, I found out about a company called
Change Heroes that was an online fundraising company. You
raised money through Change Heroes, and then a company
called Free the Children would build schools and libraries in
third-world countries with that money. All it took was
$10,000, and a schoolhouse could be built! Brilliant, I
thought. Therefore, I began asking friends and family if they
wanted to donate so we could build a school in Nicaragua. As
you can tell from the rest of this book, my friends and family
are incredible people. So, of course, we raised the money!
Thirty-five awesome people joined me in donating to this
fantastic cause. Not only did we raise $10,000, we raised over

$11,000! *In a month*! That school was built in El Trapiche, Nicaragua. Many people who are involved with the writing of this book, and who were part of my team at the U of A and Glenrose Hospitals, were a part of that project, and I am so thankful for their support.

DAVID RABORN

AGE: 29   SHERWOOD PARK, ALBERTA

BUILT A SCHOOL IN NICARAGUA

WITH 36 FRIENDS   WINTER 2015

RAISED $11,260.35

FRIENDS AND FAMILY CAME TOGETHER FOR AN AMAZING CAUSE, AND I AM EXTREMELY PROUD OF WHAT WE WERE ABLE TO DO IN SUCH A SHORT AMOUNT OF TIME!

CHANGE HEROES

Proof that my friends and I built a school in Nicaragua!

Something that I'm also very proud of doing happened on September 10th, 2016: I got back on the bike and rode in the first-ever Glenrose Hospital Foundation Courage Ride for Rehab. We rode the almost-60km around Pigeon Lake, just south of Edmonton, Alberta, and we raised over $20,000 for the Glenrose Hospital! I'm now on the committee for that Ride, and I'm excited to help grow it from the 50 riders to over a hundred in 2017, and hopefully we'll raise over a million bucks this year. ;)

My life has been very rewarding over the past five years since my bike accident. I'm not about to say it's been easy, however. As I had a very traumatic head injury, I've had to deal with all of the issues that come with that. I've had a lot of trouble sleeping, but after all these years, that is slowly getting better. I've also had two seizures. My first one was while I was working in the Student Accessibility Services office at the University of Alberta a couple of years ago, and my last one was in November of 2016. I had to rely on everyone around me to drive me around, as your license gets suspended when you have a seizure. That's the hardest part, losing my independence on both occasions. The first time it was for five months, and the last time was for three months. Luckily for me, I work with my dad, and we are together for a lot of the time anyways.

I'd like to stress the importance of having a positive attitude when it comes to recovery. I try to have a smile on my face and have positive people around me at all times. After my accident, it seemed as if there was no hope.

But there is always hope.

Never lose your persistence. No matter how dire your situation, have faith. For me, I have faith in Jesus Christ. He is love, and He will never leave you if you let Him in. I was given zero chance of survival, but here I am. Living, loving, enjoying life, and thriving. In this life, there will always be challenges, and it is never a smooth ride. Find a supportive community and get involved with them. You never know when you'll need their support.

Bob, Connie, and Robbie Lloyd visiting me at the Glenrose.

My brother, and friends from Calgary helped me support the Movember fundraiser for prostate cancer. ;)

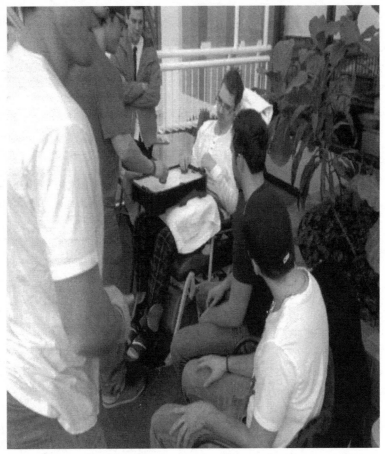

Here I am schooling Rob Cote at air hockey again...

Friends and family making the best out of a bad situation.

When we presented the Beards for Broborn cheque to the U of A Hospital. Steffie Williams (centre), Kevin Meleskie (right)

My dad, Dr. Wayne Raborn (left) and Julian Marchand (right)

Amazing friends. Lauren Dary (bottom left), Shane Leman (top left), Janet Mador (centre), Brett Mador (top right), and Neal Dary (bottom right)

Interview in fall of 2016, promoting the Glenrose Ride for Courage with former MP Laurie Hawn (left) and Mike Sobel (right)

My team for the ride! Brett Mador (Navy shirt, left), David Raborn (Canada Jersey), Ashley Brosda (centre), Sam Dehod (yellow jacket), Stefan Dehod (right)

After the ride with the best parents in the world! Wayne and Diane Raborn

25. SEQUENTIAL FACEBOOK POSTS

Introducing the Facebook Group Posts From the Group:
David Raborn' Updates and Prayers

- David Raborn, B. Comm

In most situations, having a team beside and behind you makes things easier. However, when you are battling for your life, this team concept is absolutely essential—especially in my case, where I was not able to speak up or make decisions for my own well-being.

My team, Team David as they called themselves, was incredible. In this day and age, news can spread rapidly through the Internet and especially social media. Team David used a Facebook group called "David Raborn: Updates and Prayers," Twitter, and even a website called www.beardsforbroborn.com (which is unfortunately no longer live) to get news to people interested in how I was doing. Adam Tuckwood started the Facebook group, but my brother, Taylor Raborn, provided a majority of the updates. At its peak, it had over 700 subscribers. That's a pretty big team!

I'm providing you all with some of the most vital posts, and some well wishes from my "squad." These posts will give you a perspective on what a rollercoaster ride my friends and family went through. You'll also see the widespread love, hope, and prayers that were fundamental to my survival. They are sequential, so you'll watch the story unfold if you read through them.

Please note that this segment is intentionally unedited, so please forgive any errors in spelling or grammar. I didn't want to change anything, instead keeping it as it was at the time.

Adam Tuckwood
October 4, 2011
Hey everyone.
Just a quick little update. I was in to see David today. (He)
Looks good. It's nice to see David again and he has been
making those baby steps. I told him about all the good wishes
people have been sending him and all the support that is here
for him. I told him how every time I look this group has
grown. There is one thing I want to bring up for those of you
able to visit. I know it's obvious, but working in a hospital i
know how easy it is for people to forget when they are in to
see someone they care about. We all know David is going
through the fight of his life right now, and I know we all want
to take as much burden away from him as we can. One little
thing you can do is to make sure you, and the people you are
around most, feel healthy when you come in, and to make
sure you wash your hands on the way in to see him. By
making sure we're healthy and clean when we see him we
can help prevent giving him anything else to fight. Keep it up
guys. Keep the prayers coming.

Taylor Raborn
October 4, 2011
Dear Team David:

A Tuesday update for all of you.

Before I get started, I took a gander at the 'Beards for
Broborn' shirt and I'm extremely impressed. I'd wear that V-
neck regardless because it looks so dang cool, but to wear it
(along with my haggard red-colored beard) in support of my
brother David is something that will give me a lot of pride.

163

Mad props to Steffie, Kevin and the team at Spin Ink for putting this together. The Team David shirts sound dope as well. Count me in for both.

David's condition is about the same as yesterday, but, like yesterday, he's a made a few improvements.

First, David was off the ventilator yesterday for over 12 hours. They are taking him off in spurts so that he can have a chance to rest, but even when they do so he's trying to breathe over it, which is a good sign. Every time he goes back on the ventilator he's given some sedation so his breathing rate slows down.

Second, his face and specifically the tissue around his eyes have lost much of their puffiness, or edema. He looks a lot more like David, and his eyes are opening for longer periods and look more active when they do. He's starting to blink his eyes as well, and his facial expressions look more like the ones we're used to seeing from him.

As Aunt Caroline mentioned yesterday in a note, we cannot know what David is able to hear or comprehend, but when we are in his presence we talk to him, not about him, so that he is included in the dialog. We also speak with pauses so that he can process what we're saying if he can hear right now.

Time and patience are going to be two key elements here, and we're looking for signs of improvement every day. As I mentioned earlier, I promise to give you a report at least once a day.

Before I sign off, I want to tell you that Bob and Robbie Lloyd came by the unit to see David today. Like all of us, they are concerned about David and wanted to show their support. When they walked in the hospital they weren't even wearing their Superman capes, but they were nonetheless recognized as the heroes they truly are.

My thanks cannot do justice, but thank you to both of you for what you did. None of David's recovery would be taking place without your brave acts of selflessness.

Let's keep the positive energy flowing for David!

Faithfully yours,
Taylor

Di Raborn
October 4, 2011
Hi everyone! It is 'quiet time' now between 2:30 and 4:30pm. This is the first time I have been on this wonderful site. I wasn't sure how I'd handle it, actually. But, it is good for me to be on and I thought I'd post that. Thank you, Taylor!! It means so much! Thank you Adam! Thanks to all for your love and support. It has been a God-send! To cool auntie C: I'm wearing the colorful prayer shawl you made; I can feel the prayers it was knit with! To all who are praying for David, I am soo grateful. I will now come and 'check in' often! Oh, I have decided to place scotch-tape on my inner left arm and magic- mark it with Philippians 4:13 since that is what is written on Dave's inner left arm. "Raise up your left arm, David, and look at it!!" Love and healing blessings, momma

165

Shaun Brandt

October 5, 2011

Hey All!

So in support of Kevin Meleskie's great idea (Beards for Broborn), Cam Service and I have decided to compile this awesome approach into something David can see quickly and easily when he wakes. For this, we've created beardsforbroborn.com

Lets be honest, this is going to be an Internet phenomenon. What we are asking is that you all send in photos of your beard, or rapidly growing leg hair, or just a photo of David Raborn that you love, and we will post it on the site. Please write a few short sentences for David to read with the picture for us to post with it. Our hope is to have this site looking like an endless collage of memories that can serve as an inspiration to David through his recovery process, just as he has inspired all of us.

Please e-mail your photo(s) to info@onstcreative.com with a few sentences describing your photo and we will do our best to get them all up in a timely manner. Spread this site like wildfire, and lets make David a photo album that he can remember forever! Thank you all for your continued love and support through this difficult time.

Taylor Raborn

October 5, 2011

Dear Team David:

I'm sorry for posting later in the day than usual.

As far as David's condition is concerned, today was a slow news day. He didn't move forward very much, but he didn't

166

regress either. However, there are some good signs that I want to share.

First, his medical team gave him his first drink of water through his PEG tube (his stomach tube), as they are preparing him to drink this way. To this point his fluids were provided through his IV line. A small step but one in the right direction.

Second, his eye and facial movements have become more frequent. Several visitors reported seeing his mouth move, which is the first time this has happened since David fell into a coma 13 days ago.

David's medical team continues to monitor and manage his electrolyte and fluid balance, particularly his sodium levels, which is not unusual for injuries of this nature.

This may seem to some like slow progress, but we must remember that 13 days is not long for brain injuries, and David is moving in the right direction every day.

We are going to stay united, strong and hopeful every day as David recovers, bit by bit!

Sincerely,

Taylor

PS: Kudos to Kevin and Stef for putting together some fierce T-shirt designs for Team David. Make sure you email team.broborn@gmail.com by Friday at midnight to place your orders for the first run of shirts!

Caroline Ramsey Musselwhite

October 5, 2011

My friend Mary Caldwell has giving some positive insights. She's a very skilled speech-language pathologist, who has worked on rehab teams with people who had 'closed head trauma.' She tells me that David being a athlete in multiple sports is very positive for several reasons:

• as we know, he started this journey in excellent physical condition, always a plus
• she reports that athletes make a better recovery, because they are goal-oriented, strong, used to 'coming back' etc (P.S. she notes that spoiled people do the worst) • she also noted that as a multi-sport athlete, David has developed ambidextrous skills, which lead to better synaptic connections throughout the brain
So keep the faith, Team David - lots of reasons for optimism!!

Ka Be

October 7, 2011

I can't wait for the moment Dave wakes up and thinks...."What's with all the beards?"

Taylor Raborn

October 6, 2011

Dear Team David:

A short but upbeat Thursday update for all of you.

First, remember to send in your first-run T-shirt orders to team.broborn@gmail.com before midnight on Friday. Those are some pretty nice designs, so be first on your block (if you live on one) to have these shirts.

After a few days of plateau, we have some very positive news

168

about David.

He is showing signs of consciousness! This is huge and is a big step forward. For much of the day David has his eye open (his left eye more frequently than his right), and he's been tracking visitors with it. He also appears to be communicating with visitors using eye blinks, and made a partial smile to our Dad when he told him that we were going to bring his pet dog Pokey to the unit to see him.

To give you some perspective, David was a 3 or 4 on the Glasgow coma scale on Saturday night. Today he's an 11 or 12. That's real improvement, and the signs that he has cognitive awareness are really encouraging.

Also, gone are stereotyped posturing movements (shrugging his shoulders with stiff arms was one) that we saw last week. That we don't see those means that his higher brain areas are predominating as they do in you or I.

We need to be patient, but we also need to celebrate when we encounter victories like this.

During the day David is being stimulated using appropriate music, spoken word, smell, touch and visual signals in an effort directed by professional rehabilitation scientists, including his Aunt Caroline. No Jay-Z for him just yet, but we'll get there!

Keep the immense amounts of love coming for David!

With all my gratitude,
Taylor

Shaun Brandt

October 7, 2011

"Beards for Broborn" is growing each day, including Taylor
Raborn's first beard pic! But we need more submissions.
Remember, this site isn't just for beards. It's for any photos
that you wanna post of David Raborn, and leave him a little
message with it!

Taylor Raborn

October 8, 2011

Dear Team David:

A Saturday update for all of you.

First, I need to make mention of the T-shirts that have
arrived: they look incredible! (See the photo that Stef posted
earlier to see the 'Beards for Broborn shirts in action).
Between the three t-shirt designs, there have been 120 shirt
orders made, and I'm sure more will be on the way. A big
thanks to Stef, Kevin, and the people at Spin Ink for putting
all of this together. Bravo!

Before I go any further I also need to mention a true act of
generosity put on by some of David's friends yesterday
evening. For those of you not from Canada, this weekend
marks Canadian Thanksgiving, a time that families will get
together to share each others' company and remember the
things that they are thankful for.

To my parents' surprise, a group led by Leah Karch brought
Thanksgiving to the 4th floor atrium in the hospital where
our family has been staying most of the day to be near David.
They put together a wonderful spread, including turkey and

pumpkin pie, and everyone ate and enjoyed each others' company for a few hours. The family was truly moved by the kindness and generosity. On behalf of my family, thank you to all who put this event on.

Now for David's condition:
David remains about the same as he was since Thursday evening. His eyes, particularly his left eye, opens spontaneously and often tracks visitors around the room. He has been off of the ventilator for several days now, which is excellent news. He does get tired easily, and my parents are working to get him a regular sleep-wake schedule. Another excellent sign is that David's medical team plans to move him to the step-down unit within the Neuro ICU, a sign that he has made strides in his recovery. This morning, because he hemoglobin was low, David was given a blood transfusion. (In case you were interested, his blood type is Awesome).

After reading through the published literature on head injuries, for an accident of this severity David's recovery is on schedule. We hope he continues to make progress and that he wakes up soon. Your support has really been integral to this, and although this is the most difficult Thanksgiving our family has celebrated, we are truly Thankful to have such kind and devoted friends and family.
Thank you for all that you've done for us on behalf of David.

With all my thanks,
Taylor

Taylor Raborn
October 9, 2011

171

Dear Team David:

An update for you all this Thanksgiving Sunday.
Regarding David's condition, the past 24 hours have been a
bit of a roller-coaster ride.
After his blood transfusion was completed yesterday
afternoon, David was moved to a step-down unit within the
neuro ICU. It was a pretty comfortable spot for David, and it
even had a television so he could watch sports!

However, overnight and this morning it was determined that
David has developed a bronchial infection, and he was moved
again into an isolation unit within the neuro ICU while he
fights it off. This is a gown-and-gloves area where only his
parents will be able to visit him.

This is disappointing, but we must remain hopeful: after all,
David has already fought off one infection, and they are
giving him the strongest antibiotic possible as well.
This shows us that despite the progress that David has made,
he remains vulnerable to setbacks of this type. Once he's
fought this off we all can focus on him recovering from his
head injury.
You are all aware from yesterday's post that David had to
receive a blood transfusion because his hemoglobin levels
were low. This is a great opportunity for me to stress the
importance of donating to your local blood bank. I am going
to give blood this week, and I encourage you to do the same.
Let's show solidarity with David by pledging to give blood
while giving life to those who are in need. You never know-
the blood you give could save someone's brother.

172

It has been a very difficult Thanksgiving, but I write this note filled with appreciation and gratitude to all of you for the support you've shown David and the Raborn family. My family remains strong and united and is extremely thankful for our friends and family.

Let's keep the messages of love for David coming as he faces down this infection.

Happy Thanksgiving,
Taylor

Taylor Raborn
October 9, 2011
Team David:
Further to my previous post, let's see how many units of blood we can donate this month on David's behalf. David is a humanitarian, but also a competitive guy and it would please him to no end knowing that we were giving life to others in his name by donating blood!

Di Raborn
October 10, 2011
Please pray for a healing, solid sleep throughout the night for David as it is his first night breathing completely on his own with no assistance~Thank you.

Taylor Raborn
October 12, 2011 ·

A postcard I received from David Raborn the day of the accident. The most precious thing I own. Can't wait to read the next one you write me D! Until then I'm going to honor you with my whole strength.

Proudly your big brother,
Taylor

The postcard that Taylor received the day of my accident.

Taylor Raborn
October 10, 2011
Dear Team David:

An update for all of you on this Thanksgiving Monday. After yesterday's more downbeat tone, today's news on David's condition is more positive.

As I told you in yesterday's update, David's doctors found that he had a bronchial infection, so he was moved to an isolation unit within the neuro ICU as he fights it off. Thanks to this measure and treatment with powerful antibiotics, David's temperature is now under control, and he seems to be doing better today. It will take about 5 days at a minimum to clear this infection, but we're collectively less worried now than we were last night.

We had some good news today- David's tracheotomy was 'plugged', so now David is breathing through his mouth for the first time since the accident. This came unexpectedly for us, and is definitely a small victory.

David appears to be more responsive today than usual. He got to watch the Thanksgiving Day football games, and seemed to track the action and focus with his eyes, especially now since he's wearing his glasses. He does get tired easily and his new private room has helped him get better sleep than usual.

After our family met with David's neurosurgeon today, we have good news about his CT scans: his brain, which had shifted to the right immediately after the accident, is now positioned precisely where it should be in his cranium. His brain swelling continues to come down and there is no reason for another surgery.

Even though he's still fighting an infection, we're positive about the direction David moved in today and anticipate more improvement tomorrow.

You all are one of the main things we are thankful for this Thanksgiving Monday. Your support continues to give us strength and hope.

Let's stay positive for David this week: it just might be the week he starts to wake up!!

With all my gratitude. Taylor

Di Raborn
October 12, 2011
I just wanted to thank everyone for all your love and support. It has been amazing and so appreciated. I truly feel God's mercy through all of your wonderful and caring, outpouring of Spirit. It has been uplifting to say the least. Everyone is officially a 'Southerner' as I have never seen so much food!! And, as for the personal contact, it has been awesome. Although I wish we could have just thrown a Fall Barbeque, God's ways are not always our ways and I do feel His loving Presence holding us up throughout this storm. Your prayers, visits, kindnesses and love have touched us deeply. Thank you from all of the Raborns. Philippians 4:13 for Dave

Taylor Raborn
October 13, 2011 · Iowa City, IA, United States
Dear Team David:
A Wednesday update for all of you. I apologize for not posting sooner.

The last two days have been positive overall for David, although it hasn't been entirely a smooth ride.

When I last posted I told you that David's infection was under control and that he was staying in the isolation room in the neuro ICU while it cleared.

For the moment, David remains in this room, and the infection is still under control, but his medical team thinks that he's improved enough over the past 20 days to warrant him being transferred out of the neuro ICU entirely and into the neurology ward of the hospital.

We must see this for what it is: a real piece of good news. In the midst of setbacks here and there we can sometimes miss the big picture - that for the first half of his stay in the hospital his doctors were worried simply for his survival. Now, as of this moment David is stable and will move into the neurology ward in the next day or so. This is true progress!

I will keep you posted on this when his move does happen, and how to get there to visit (it will still be at the University of Alberta Hospital) if you're in the Edmonton area.

David's face, so swollen with what's called facial edema and with large black eyes, now looks as normal as it's been since the accident. This is not just a cosmetic change: it also signals that his water balance is being regulated correctly. David now opens both eyes, including his right eye, for extended periods of time, and both pupils' track visual stimuli including his visitor, the television and even a mirror.

David does become tired quite easily, and sleeps in periods during the day.

Fortunately, he is able to get more restful sleep in his current location in the isolation room. The neurology ward is also quiet relative to the neuroICU so his upcoming move should help him here as well.

I can report that there are some small signs suggesting that he may be waking up, but it is difficult to be sure until we have more evidence. Once that evidence does come, you all will hear it from me straightaway.

We all have to continue to be patient, and as positive as ever. Let's end the week strong, just like we hope David does!

Keep the messages of love and encouragement coming. I have no doubt that David will read them one day in the future, and they will power him forward just as your support for our family have helped us to soldier through each day.

Yours sincerely,
Taylor

Colleen D'Something (my High School English teacher living in Austrailia)
October 14, 2011
David,
You will sooo appreciate this. So, I'm at camp with 39 year 9 girls. We're all sitting around and someone notices the hair on my leg. I ask them if they're missing their dogs - we've been away from 'civilization' for a week - the last two days

without showers, digging our own toilets in the bush, living in home made tents. I offer to let them pet my leg hair. One brave girl takes me up on the offer. "Wow," she says, "it actually does feel like a dog." LOL! Thanks to you dear David, bringing comfort to people all over the globe 😊;) Praying for you buddy! Love Mrs. I xo

Di Raborn
October 14, 2011
So.... this is a 'halleluiah moment'! Went in to see Dave. Rennie (Janet's friend) is his nurse today. And she has been working and talking with him and showed me how he can give the 'thumbs up' on command. As well as blink as a response. He got really tired and only did it once for me definitively but this is amazing to see.

Taylor Raborn
October 16, 2011 · Iowa City, IA, United States
Dear Team David:
It's been several days since I posted, but I want to make sure all of you are up to speed on David's condition.

The last few days were quite positive overall, but as usual there were a few setbacks mixed in.

I'll begin with the good news: as our mom Diane Raborn mentioned, on Friday David gave his first definitive sign of consciousness, giving a thumbs-up signal on command to his charge nurse and also squeezing her hand. Before, we had only hunches that David was responding, but nothing solid. This is simply wonderful, as it tells us that David is 'in there'; that his cerebral cortex (grey matter) is working and capable

179

of executing at least a few tasks.

After being so deep in a coma since the accident happened, David is starting to wake up, and this is an inflection point in this process.

We should all be excited, but David still has a long way to go. I must emphasize that he doesn't respond to commands with a thumbs up very often, likely because he gets tired very easily, and sleeps for most of the day. This is the first time since I met him that I can say that David is 'weak as a kitten', but there is no doubt in my mind that this is only temporary and he'll be strong as ever someday soon. David's nurses are beginning to move him to a 'Stryker chair', a custom chair that supports him while giving him a more upright posture. We'll see him in this chair more often as he picks up strength and signs of consciousness.

I mentioned in my last post that David still had an infection, and with that an elevated temperature. He remains in the isolation room of the neuro ICU, but his infection appears to be cleared and he no longer has a temperature.

Counter intuitively, moving to the isolation room may have been a good thing for David, because it's given him the opportunity to have over a week of solid night's sleep while ensuring that he has the constant nursing care that the ICU provides.

This Friday we had a slight scare as one of David's nurses found a large blood clot in David's left lower leg, a condition known as a Deep Vein Thrombosis (DVT). While this not entirely unexpected given his extended bed rest, it could have had dire consequences were it not discovered: a part of the clot could have broken off and traveled through the bloodstream to his lungs. This would have given him what's known as a pulmonary embolism, which is bad news. A big thanks to David's nurse Rennie for catching this- we dodged a bullet!

David's clot is now being treated with a few thrombolytic drugs, which over time will break down David's clot, and his blood is being monitored closely.
Another bit of good news is that David is breathing on his own, through his mouth. It wasn't too long ago that he was breathing using a respirator, so this is also true progress.

Like all of you, I am hoping for David's best week yet. I will give you updates as David shows further signs of waking up. We must remember that at the moment he is still in a coma, but has a higher score than he did on Thursday.

I am so thankful for the many messages of support for David last week. Let's give him even more love this week- we are united as a team for him every single step of the way!

Appreciatively,
Taylor

Lauren Dary
October 17, 2011
Dave - I keep thinking about August when you and Tay arrived at Elmhirst Resort for B & J's wedding extravaganza. I

saw you from down the street as you were going into your cabin and said to Kaylin, " DAVE'S HERE!!" and just started sprinting down the road to see you! Barging into your cabin and gave you a big hug. I miss you so much. I can't wait for the day soon when I can do this sequence all over again. All my love and support, bro!

Adam John
October 18, 2011
Davey, I know you were pushing me to get the quotes I had been posting on my wall to twitter and link to FB and back to twitter and...Well you knew more about that then I did... But now that you have gathered 600 people in one location I thought this would be your ideal place to share the positive thoughts... Good things bud!

"You can do anything you wish to do, have anything you wish to have, be anything you wish to be."
-- Robert Collier

Connie Moulins Lloyd
October 18, 2011 · New Sarepta
Dave, my husband and son were the fellas that found you that fateful evening. They and I are very excited to meet you under better circumstances.
Have to say, you gave us all quite a scare, but you also introduced us to this wonderful group of people who love you very much!

We are rooting for you all day, every day and appreciate your brother's very in depth updates.

Looking forward to meeting you and swapping stories!! I bet you have plenty to share.
Keep fighting!!

- All the Lloyds.

Taylor Raborn
October 19, 2011
David's watching the Cards play in the World Series right now!
Let's go Redbirds!

Lauren Dary
October 19, 2011 · Calgary
I am loving all of the beard pictures on the http://beardsforbroborn.com site! David, you are going to absolutely LOVE this. Some of those beards are delicious. I won't name names, as to not pump up anyone's egos. But I need to put this out there: Ladies - why are you leaving me hanging as the sole provider of a leg-hair photo? I don't mind, but I know David is going to be impressed if we can get more up! Do it Do it Do it!

Ka Be
October 20, 2011
I'm so excited to hear Taylor's news!
I had the COOLEST dream last night that I wanted to share. At the hospital, there were hundreds of Dave's friends and family all hanging out in the common area where his family is. There were actual bleachers set up full of people who all

had little signs, face paint, body paint, just all out. People were sitting around at tables playing cards and talking and laughing; they were all camping out because somehow everyone knew that Dave was going to be waking up any minute. Such a random but awesome dream that everyone was literally THERE waiting for him to wake up- ready to jump, and cheer, and scream with happiness when he did, just like we were all at another football game watching him play!

I have awesome, awesome energy about today and I'm sending all of it to you David Raborn!!!

Taylor Raborn
October 20, 2011
Dear Team David:
I hope this update finds you all well - it's certainly been a good week so far for David.

In my last update on Sunday night, David had given a thumbs-up signal a few times, but was still in the neuro ICU being treated for a bronchial infection. I can say that he has made real progress since then.

During the past four days, David's temperature has fallen, his vitals look excellent and a few hours ago his medical team took the step of moving him OUT (!!!) of the neuro ICU and across the hall to the Neurology ward in the University of Alberta Hospital (4A20), where David now has his own private room.

On its own, this is a real victory for David and all of us. To be moved out of Intensive Care is a sign that he's turned the corner and is on the beginnings of a road to recovery. We

184

need to celebrate every small victory along this path and this is one of them.

But there's more! Yesterday David, visited by a few friends and family, moved his left arm about 5 inches and across towards his midline. He did this last night and again this morning. This is a sure sign that he beginning to coordinate conscious movements, which tells us that his brain is continuing to heal. He is also able to squeeze people's hands and looks more alert each day. We think that he is trying to mouth words, but cannot be sure a) what he's attempting to communicate in this fashion and b) if what's he's trying to mouth is meaningful. These efforts are evidence of progress but they also make him very tired, so he's been sleeping a lot.

Our mom Diane has developed a communications system with David involving him tightly closing his eyes so that he can respond in the affirmative to yes/no questions. Using this method, he has indicated that he knows what the current day and time is from a set of choices given to him. Our David is certainly 'in there', and now we wait for the swelling of his brain that was brought on by this injury to continue to subside so that we see more and more of him! This process takes time and is highly unpredictable. That we are seeing steady progress should buoy our sprits. To make it clear, David remains in a coma but his score has increased, so he's 'more awake' than before.

All of this is excellent news and we are hopeful that we will see more progress soon. Now that David is in the Neurology ward, it is much easier for him to be attended to by rehabilitation specialists: occupational therapists, physical therapists and speech language pathologists. These professionals are absolutely vital to his recovery and we are fortunate to have some of Canada's best at the University of Alberta Hospital.

There will be lots of rehabilitation to be completed, but David is a fighter and he has the most incredible team behind him: all of you, Team David.

Our family could not be more happy or more thankful for your support for David and us.

Let's cheer this positive milestone and push David toward the next one!

With my deepest gratitude,
Taylor

Jenny Mador
October 21, 2011
These posts are so encouraging every time. Thank You Taylor!! They bring me to tears..not because I am sad, but because my heart is literally attached to my emotions and means I am Soooo HAPPY our David is with us and making wonderful progress each day. There isn't a day I miss a post, or forget to send you hopeful, positive thoughts. I know you are strong and so smart Dave! Keep going! We are with you every step of the way! Xoxo

Stef Williams
October 20, 2011
Dave: You've got mail!

Team David: To add to Taylor Raborn's great news of this weeks progression... I've got one more announcement to make. YOUR SHIRTS ARE HERE! The guys at Spin Ink made it happen... Over 100 shirts on rush order especially for our team.

I don't think it could have been any better timing... I believe that all of this coming together is a sign. Keep sharing your strength and good vibes with David Raborn and his family! He's a man of many talents and continues to shine through. Let's reflect all of the positive energy right back where it belongs at this time - to him... Please be patient with Kevin Meleskie, Adam Tuckwood and I as we embark on an adventure to distribute the "team jerseys" to everyone. We will be in touch ASAP with arrangements for pick-up and donation information. (Check your emails!) Thanks again for all of your support - I think we're going to have to get a "C" stitched on to a shirt for our team captain... "A" will have to go to the best beard. Let's all hope for good news from here on in 😊

Beards for Broborn T-shirts arrive!

Wendy Van Drunen (teacher from Jr. High School)
October 23, 2011 · Sherwood Park
Every Sunday since your accident I have been going for a run
in the river valley and sending the power, strength and
beauty of the river to you! Every Sunday has been sunny - a
good sign. Been thinking about you David as I walk the halls
at Haythorne - hoping you wake up soon. - Mrs. V

Kate Walline
October 24, 2011
Hey handsome, I'm beyond glad to hear such positive

updates about how tough of a fighter you are. You continue to amaze me each day with your resiliency my friend. It's 4am and for some reason, I woke up thinking back to this summer about how I was lucky enough to get to work at the 'check in' station at NBC with you. The very first station that all the excited, nervous, old, and new campers come to on their first day of camp. There was clearly a reason you were asked to man that particular station. Maybe it was because your name was randomly pulled from a hat to man it, but I like to think it was because of something greater. You could immediately see the excitement in each child's face after they got a big welcome high five from coach Dave, and the ease in their voice and face after you looked at them with your kind big blue eyes and flashed them one of your infamous smiles. You immediately made a positive impact on their experience with such little effort really needed on your part. You have an innate ability to change lives with your humble demeanor, kind eyes, and friendly smile. Keep fighting the fight so you can keep touching the lives of all that are lucky enough to encounter you my friend ♥

Megan Schellenberg
October 25, 2011
A few of us went to watch the first period of the Oilers game with David and it was amazing! He looked awesome and was even sporting his own Oilers jersey! Go David Go! ☺

Cherie Hunchak
October 25, 2011
The LORD is my strength and my shield;
My heart trusted in Him, and I am helped;

Therefore my heart greatly rejoices,
And with my song I will praise Him. Psalm 28:7

Stef Williams
October 25, 2011
Team Broborn! You guys rule! Tonight's turn out for t-shirt pick up was unbelievable. Dave, your support is never ending - Everybody had something positive to say about you when they stopped by tonight - You're in everybody's thoughts! (Even the strangers at the tables next to us were cheering you on!) We had the pleasure of meeting new faces and catching up with old friends.. Thanks for coming out and showing your support for Team David!

There will be another opportunity for pick-up in the very near future - stay tuned for Kevin's message!

Kevin Meleskie
October 26, 2011 · Edmonton
Just a heads up.... Steffie and I will be at the Starbucks on 109th and Jasper this Saturday from 2-5pm! Come get your shirts! Also, you can donate money to the cause by email money transferring to team.broborn@gmail.com. Were not in a position to give tax receipts but your money will go directly to the u of a neurology unit that treat our buddy Dave.
Cheers,
Kevin

Di Raborn
October 27, 2011
If Dave sits up and recites the military phonetic alphabet

forwards and backwards, sings 'If your ears hang low, do they wobble to and fro.."; "Skinamarinky Dinky Do..."; or says: " I think I can, I think I can " please do not think it strange.

Kevin Meleskie
October 27, 2011 · Edmonton
Just an FYI: the shirts being sold at these designated locations and times have all been ordered and are spoken for. If there is a lot of interest we will so another run of printing. You can still donate to the cause by email money transferring to team.broborn@gmail.com. We will let you know if at the end of this campaign there are still shirts that haven't been picked up and make them available to the late comers!

Lauren Dary
October 28, 2011
Top three moments of 2011: Neal marrying me, David squeezing my hand, seeing the foo fighters live while wearing our team Broborn shirts.

Taylor Raborn
October 29, 2011 · Coralville, IA, United States
Today at Foote Field at 1PM the University of Alberta Golden Bears will take on the U of Saskatchewan Huskies in their final game of the season.

This will also mark the last game of Bears' QB Julian Marchand, who has been as strong a supporter of Team David as anyone. Julian and David have been close friends for several years, and were teammates in Calgary.

Julian is also the only person I know to have consistently held the upper hand with David in 1 on 1 basketball. You'll have to ask him how he pulled that off- I'm still scratching my head. [this is a false statement, as Julian is an amazing friend, but quite delusional sometimes ;)]

On the night of the accident Julian stayed up all night with David's parents at the U of A Hospital, and has been a source of a lot of strength for myself personally and our entire family since that time.
If you're able, do stop down to Foote Field to cheer on Julian and the Golden Bears. I know he would appreciate your support and also know he's capable of some magic on the field (see last year's playoff game vs. U of S).

If David were able to watch, he would be there too.

On behalf of the Raborn Family and Team David, Go Julian- we love you!

Di Raborn
October 29, 2011
Last Saturday, Nick, "the Scholar" Dehod, and Momma, "the Hype" Raborn played the last chess game in the best 2 out of 3 championship match in David's room. Nick said he was playing for Dave. I was playing for Dave as well; but for an additional 'something': a group 'helmet photo' since Dave must wear a helmet until yet another surgery takes place to replace his missing bone. As well, a helmet saved Dave's life. It was a challenging game for both. The 'Hype' was down to 2 pawns and a queen. Squeaking out a win, the 'Hype' is glad to report that a group photo of helmet supporters will be in the offing. Thanks to Nick, "the Scholar" for a stellar match!

Lisa Holowaychuk

October 30, 2011

D- Not a day goes by that I don't pray, think of you, send you, your family and friends my love and wishes. I know I will come back at Christmas and we will share a good laugh and a steaming cup of tea! Be strong. As you inspire us all, by just being YOU. Your smile and laugh light up this world, and we are ready for it! Any day now. xoxo – L

Di Raborn

October 30, 2011

Prayer truly is one of the most studied practices in medicine. Over and over it has been proven that prayer helps people heal, even if they don't pray themselves but are prayed for by others. Prayer aids healing. Thank you for your continued prayers.

Taylor Raborn

October 30, 2011

Dear Team David:

I hope this note finds you all well. It's been just over a week since I provided all of you with an update, and there is much to catch you up on.

In my last update, about a week ago, David had just been moved to the Neurology Unit of the University of Alberta Hospital from the neuro ICU. This was undoubtedly a good move, because it allows him to have closer access to the excellent rehabilitation professionals on site.

I'll begin by saying that from a physical standpoint, David is doing as well as he has been since the accident. His tracheotomy has been plugged, so he is breathing normally through his mouth as you or I do. On a few occasions since moving to his new unit David had a tracheotomy tube re-inserted so that he could breathe a little easier, but this hasn't been necessary for several days now.

This is good news, and allows his medical team focus on David's neurological recovery. On this front, David has been making progress as well. He is becoming more active, and is able to move both hands within a limited range. When he's awake and has enough energy, he gives his nurses and visitors hand signals, like 'thumbs up' or more recently an 'ok' circle with his thumb and index finger. His face is starting to show more expression, and I have seen faint smiles on several occasions, as have many others. This morning, for the first time, David turned his head using his neck- a big step. The evidence suggests that he is able to understand much of what is said to him, and his Aunt Caroline is working with his family and medical team to bring an innovative communication board to his bedside. To this end, our parents got David an iPad so he can start using that device to read and (hopefully soon) communicate.

There have been glimpses of even more exciting milestones: yesterday David's nurses and his mother say that David was trying to speak to them, but the sounds he was making were not able to be deciphered. This is great news, as it suggests that verbal communication from David may be on the horizon.

This week marks the first that David has been seen by

194

Rehabilitation specialists. They have worked at his bedside to improve his range of motion, especially in his legs and feet. His mother Diane Raborn has been a huge part of this as well, reading to him, playing him classical music and rubbing his feet to promote blood flow there. His father Wayne Raborn has also been a big part of this, reading him the news every day, and even more importantly, this week's issue of Sports Illustrated.

His medical team has started moving him during the day to a Stryker chair, which helps him work on his body posture and gives him a more natural, upright position to be in.

Support from all of you continues to pour in, and we cannot thank all of you enough for it. We are in awe of it just as we are collectively in awe of David's fighting spirit.

None of us can say how long David's road to recovery will be, but I can say that he will have an army of devoted supporters in all of you along the way, and for that myself and my family remain deeply grateful.

Let's all cheer David on as he begins a new week- I have a feeling that he is going to show even more progress!

Yours sincerely,
Taylor

Taylor Raborn
October 30, 2011
David's business partners Shaun and Cam stopped by to tell him about their progress with Giraffe!

Which reminds me- send them your beard photo updates for Beards for Broborn (info@onstcreative.com)

My partners, Shaun Brandt (left) and Cam Service (right) at the hospital.
We were working on a startup together before I got into the accident.

Di Raborn

November 1, 2011

David was 'decantilated' today~ a 5 minute procedure to remove his 'trach'! Now, if only, his hiccups would stop!! [I'm told the hiccups were awful in the hospital...]

Veronica May

November 1, 2011

Sporting our awesome David t-shirts on the new set of CTV Morning Live. Love you David, we think about you all day, everyday!!

CTV reporter and broadcaster Veronica Jubinville (left), Andrew West (middle) and Alison West (right) sporting their Broborn shirts!

Lisa Mol
November 1, 2011 · Edmonton
Dear David,
I would like to arrange to bring a guitar up to your room along with a couple of singers and serenade you! What do you think?

Brianna Stratton
November 2, 2011
thought of you the whole week at Halifax Pop Explosion (150 bands in 5 days in Halifax)..sooo many amazing hipster beards. best concert of the festival was Dan Mangan and friends performing in St. Matthews United Church, especially his grand finally when he went unplugged and sang from the pues. video doesn't quite do it justice but had to share cause

you would have loved it! thoughts and prayers with you always, keep on keepin on Davey boy. Love you!

Darren Danyk
November 3, 2011
Hey, kid. We've never met met and I don't know you, but I am friends with someone who does know you and I happened upon this group. While browsing, I could not help but be moved by the way you have affected so many lives. You truly are an inspiration. I can only hope that one day I am able to reach as many people even half as deeply as you appear to have already. Seeing the way you are loved makes me want to be a better person. I hope that I can have the pleasure of meeting you one day. Until that day comes, stay strong, kid (I'm fairly certain saying that is redundant). My prayers are with you. [I had prayers from many people like this. Thanks you all for supporting me!]

Erin Jean Burdzy
November 3, 2011 · Calgary
Dave, you are a perfect example of how simply the way you live your life can be a testament in itself. Matthew 5:16. (kudos to your family for rasing such an amazing young man!)

Stay strong, God's got some big things lined up for ya and this is all part of the journey to get you there. We may not understand but the big guy tends to know what He's doing. Jeremiah 29:11

Taylor Raborn
November 3, 2011

Dear Team David:

Today marks six weeks since the terrible accident that has temporarily stolen David from us.

I didn't commemorate two weeks, or a month, but I did choose six weeks. In celestial terms six weeks is the mere blink of an eye, but it's long enough to give us cause to look back and reflect. Fad diets often promise results in six weeks, French summer vacations are six weeks; even some condensed University terms last six weeks.
During our long friendship, David and I scarcely went more than twelve hours without communicating. Six weeks without speaking, even if I were traveling like Stanley through the depths of an unexplored territory, would have been unthinkable prior to this event.

Seeing David suffer and be incapacitated by his injuries has been, by orders of magnitude, the most excruciating thing I have ever endured. As his older brother my every impulse is to protect David from harm, and yet and I was unable to prevent or ameliorate the Harm that did come his way.

Thanks in large measure to the support of you and many others, our family's resolve remains strong, and we are prepared to walk together with David for as long as the road back proves to be. It would be lying to you if I said that my pillow is dry every night or that I fully comprehend all that has happened. But in my dark moments I lift my head from the grief and ponder where David is in the process, and it gives me hope.
By sheer good fortune, David was found at the scene on

RR223 by a Good Samaritan and hero, Bob Lloyd and his son, Robbie. After the accident, David had fallen into as deep a coma as is clinically possible. Two subsequent emergency surgeries saved his life, and the fragile first weeks after the accident he was kept alive in one of two hospitals in Canada with a neuro ICU.

Viewed from a wide angle, David's progress from those bleak early moments to this day are simply incredible. Today David is quite responsive, alert and his physical health is as strong as it's been before the accident. I am deeply grateful for this progress, and like all of you, and I very hopeful for David's continued recovery.
We must remember that for traumatic brain injuries like this one, patience is sorely needed. The human brain, the single most complex object ever studied, needs time to repair itself and to form the synaptic connections it lost, and we really cannot know what amount of time is necessary. What we do know is that David is progressing, and that is really wonderful news.

We've all endured, in effect, six weeks without David, that dynamic, bright, funny and kind young man that we love so dearly. I must remind you that it is not selfish in the least to miss the contributions he made in and to our lives- I number them daily. As he recovers, those things will return gradually, but for the time being the void remains in our lives, and denying this fact does us no great service.

I have grieved his absence by remembering specific things that David and I did together, and the myriad ways he enriched my life: the messages at unexpected times when an idea or dream struck, the excitement and curiosity that bubbled within. His fierce competitiveness yet true empathy. The rare person that you could truly dream with without fear of ridicule or doubt.

While this exercise often makes me sad, it's a reminder that David still lives inside me, even when he hasn't completely woken up.

For me, David is both counselor and confidant; alternatively muse and sage, and at times I feel like a boat without rudder or mast. But our bonds are not broken or damaged; we just lack our regular interactions. His vast archive of friendship guides me every day.

To some of you in this lovely group, David is a friend, teammate, business partner, coach, son, cousin, nephew, classmate and much more. David is here, so those relationships remain, similarly: do not mourn their loss. Instead honor what they've done for your lives, and celebrate each milestone on his path to recovery.
David is fighting every single day to restore his place in our lives.

So remember your David, keep him in your heart, and smile. Keep the flame we lit together with him alight.

The day comes when David will be strong enough to carry it aloft with us.

Kevin Meleskie
November 5, 2011 · Edmonton

Great day with Dave..scratched his head and chest, gave the ok sign, gave a fist bump, and the little weasel almost managed to take his helmet off....twice! Great work kiddo

Caroline Ramsey Musselwhite
November 5, 2011
Hi All,

I know many of you are able to visit David now that he's out of ICU - yay! Would you please share these 'guidelines' with everyone? Also, YOU can be great models for all of the medical staff working with David.

1) Always address ALL comments TO David, never ever ABOUT him. If you hear others talking about David in your hearing, please be a good model. Ex: someone says, 'Does David seem to understand you?' You respond - "Hey Dave, X is asking about how you're understanding. Remember yesterday when I talked to you about the xxx winning the game? That got a big smile. And Lauren was telling me that you gave her a big thumbs up when xxxxx."

2) Be sure not to use a 'hospital voice' (louder & kind of childish). However, people who are coming out of a coma may need more time to process. So talk at a normal intonation, but leave pauses between phrases & sentences. I call this the Processing Pause. For example, "Hey David . . . it's Jen . . . You're looking really great . . . . Did you hear about the Cards? . . . . They really pulled it off . . . I was so sure . . they

202

were going to blow it, ... but Man, what an ending!"

Hope this makes sense! Please comment if you have questions or more ideas. Remember that David IS hearing you, and your input is helping him to progress!
[Dr.] Caroline (speech-language pathologist)

Colleen D'Something
November 6, 2011
Just got the call, chapel moved ahead to today. Will be presenting: Beards for Broborn this morning to about 800 students ☺ :) Thinking of you David! Will send pics soon. C x

Shannon Raborn [My sister]
November 9, 2011
Hi David - it is a perfect blue sky day here, a bit crisp, but clear. We took Sage xc skiing (well we were skiing and she was running) on Sunday. It was freezing cold and snowing the whole time. She loved it of course! Thinking about you and wishing you a great day. Keep up the excellent work! Hugs, Shannon

Di Raborn
November 9, 2011
Just gave the hospital speech therapist, Karolin, a huge hug! She finally saw all the things we all have been seeing and was very impressed! Thanks to poppa who showed her all the games they've been playing! Dave passed with flying colours :) Now, she just needs to talk to ICAN to pass along the results and then the long wait.

Stacey Sperling

November 9, 2011 · Hue, Vietnam

Dave! I love reading how great you're recovery is going and hearing all the amazing things you are doing! Keep pushing and I can't imagine the crazy things you'll be able to do by the time I visit in December! Sending lots of love and prayers from Vietnam.

Tyne Kover

November 10, 2011

David you are so strong.. you have a lot of healing ahead of you but I know you will overcome every obstacle that may cross your path!! I believe and have faith in you!! ☺

Taylor Raborn

November 10, 2011

Dear Team David:

It's been more than a week since my last update, and what a week it's been!

Let me bring you all up to speed on how our wonderful David is doing.

At the time of my last update, David had been moved out of the neuroICU and had his own private room in the neurology wing of the hospital.

A few days thereafter David was moved to another room in neurology, this one with a roommate, and this is where he remains.

Although his physical condition remained stable, his

204

neurological and apparent cognitive progress last week was fairly slow. This week, however, is another story.

This week David's limb movements have become more animated, along with an improved range of motion. He is still bed-ridden for much of the day, but he spends longer periods of time in a special Stryker chair out in the Healing Garden or Atrium of the University of Alberta Hospital.

David seems lucid, and can nonverbally answer questions posed to him by his parents, friends or attending therapy staff. His facial expressions remain limited, but we've seen glimpses of his signature smile.

Here is a brief example of progress that he has made:

On Tuesday David, who had some dry lips, took Chap Stick from his dad, removed the cap, applied it and returned the cap to its proper place. He did this more deliberately than you or I would, but this is a very exciting example of progress with his manual dexterity.

His family and friends have seen further glimpses of progress: when he was hanging out with his father in the Healing Garden David laughed when the two were buckling up his seatbelt. Last night David took a photo of a group of his closest friends using one of their iPhones.

As I write this tonight I'm literally amazed at the progress David has made in a few short weeks. With time can expect further progress, but of course the amount that is necessary for each milestone is unpredictable, so we must be as patient as we are hopeful.

I mentioned to you that David communicates non-verbally, but he has not yet been able to speak. He has been seen mouthing words and making soft sounds, but they've been unintelligible. Communicating through speaking is the next milestone we look forward to, and it's obvious that David is working so hard to get there. We are all very excited to hear from him when he's able to talk to us!

As he continues to 'wake up' (from a clinical standpoint he'll still be in a coma until he can communicate verbally), David has been receiving important rehabilitation treatments from the Occupational, Physical, and Speech Pathlogy Therapists at the U of A Hospital. He has a great team that works with him daily and his family is there to read to him, interact with him and stimulate him during other parts of the day.
With all of the excitement during the day, David still gets quite tired. He takes several naps a day, although he does not need as much as sleep he did in the month after the accident. The only existing non-neurological medical issue that his doctors are still trying to break up his Deep Vein Thrombosis (a blood clot) in his left leg. They have it under close surveillance and are giving him the necessary drugs to manage it. That's a far cry from the laundry list of issues he had just a few weeks ago- something else to be thankful for.

Before I close, I need to tell you all how appreciative we are for your support for David. In situations like this one I'm told that interest wanes after a few weeks, but your strength has held steadfast. Words of encouragement continue to pour in from all corners of the country and globe. This has given us tremendous strength.

With his new iPad, David is now able to read the posts made in this group.
Let's shower David with love and tell him how proud we are of his progress and how much we care about him!

With love,
Taylor
Clear eyes, full hearts, can't lose.

Kevin Meleskie at The Venetian Las Vegas.
November 11, 2011 · Las Vegas, NV, United States
Wish you were here buddy; it's not the same without you
[I missed Kevin's bachelor party, and later his wedding, that I was a supposed to be a groomsman at ;(]

 Leah Milne Tuckwood
November 11, 2011
David, I just read Taylor's most recent post on your progress. Wow! We are very excited to hear how well you are doing. Aaron completed his masters recently so we were at the university of Calgary yesterday, for his convocation. I know you were a Dino at one point so I caught myself thinking of you while walking around the campus. Aaron was a proud 'bear' and I, a 'panda', so i was actually bugging Aaron about becoming a Dino. 😊 ;) Our family still prays for you and we love to hear of your amazing progress. Thanks Taylor for the great update!

Kaitie Beard
November 11, 2011
David Raborn! I am in tears as I read what Taylor just wrote about your progress! I am overjoyed by the strength you

have and the determination of everyone around you. I can't wait for you to read this post and I hope it brings that famous smile of yours to that beautiful face! I love you Dave and pray everyday for you. Xoxo

Kamry Pizzey Low
November 11, 2011
David, so excited to hear about your progress. I was visiting last Friday and since then it sounds like you've improved tons! I'm hopefully going to pop by next week sometime. Maybe you can teach me how to use my new iPhone camera well! Looks like you can take a good photo! Keep up the good work! Kamry

Veronica May
November 12, 2011
Thanks for letting us paint with you today!! loved the thumbs up and fist pound. You are doing so good, so proud of you!!
 <3

Thomas Ogilvie
November 12, 2011
Davey boy so happy to hear that you are doing as well as you are I am home tomorrow go a lot to do as I am going to Asia backpacking then moving to aus on dec 28 so much to do before I leave. I really want to see you so I am going to try my hardest to make it there tomorrow if not I give you my word you will see me before I leave. I still pray for you every day my friend my strength and live also goes your way everyday keep up the fantastic work Dave you are an inspiration to us all.

Adam John

November 13, 2011

Davey! I love reading Taylor's posts because I know they hold news of your improvement. Keep fighting hard buddy. I make decisions everyday based on what I have learned from you throughout this process. Good things, can't wait to see you next. Sending love from Amy as well.

Brennan Lafleur

November 14, 2011 · Edmonton

I've joined you in rocking a mustache buddy! Mine is significantly less manly and a little more patchy, but hey, it's the thought that counts right?

Lauren Deklerk

November 14, 2011

DAVID! I'm so jacked about how awesome you are coming along, keep up the unreal healing buddy! you're such an inspiration for me in the coaching aspect of my life and in so many areas besides that! you're amazing, heal up quick - NBC nation misses you buddy!

Kevin Meleskie

November 14, 2011 · Edmonton

Dave we made it back safely from Vegas! The first night we all rocked our beards for Broborn shirts with blazers! Your story was told to many and many people from around the world had a drink to your good health! We had a fun time and you were the topic of many conversations! Though you weren't there in body your presence was definitely felt and you were the subject of many a cheers! Love ya buddy, it wasn't the same without you but we tried our best to do what we know you would do.... make plays! Xo

Kristy Hubens
November 14, 2011 · Edmonton
Hey Buddy! You are rocking this recovery! So great to see you over the past few days, and Ill be back later this week to

deal with that moustache of yours 😊 :) Hope your feeling better and kick this cold your getting in a hurry! P.S. That signed painting of yours is going to be worth millions!!!

Taylor Fuchs
November 15, 2011
Dave! Out watching Tom Brady dominate and thinking of you. I can't wait until our next football game. I'm so thrilled with how great you are doing! Keep up the amazing work and I can't wait to see you again.

Chelsea Lunan Greene
November 15, 2011
We never stop thinking about you Dave. You are always in our hearts. As mine and Adam's 1st wedding anniversary fast approaches, we are filled with beautiful memories of sharing that day with you. Can't wait to see you again!

Colette Meek Haslam
November 16, 2011 - near Sherwood Park

Dave, watching you write my name (under your hand) and answer questions on who's your favorite NFL team and who

210

you went w/ to the grand canyon when you guys came to visit was honestly the most amazing thing I've seen. It so so great to see how much progress you're making and to be able to get inside your head a little after all these weeks!!! Keep fighting, seeing you get better every week is so inspiring! Can't wait to see where you're at next time I see you again in a few weeks!

Caroline Ramsey Musselwhite
November 15, 2011
HELP NEEDED!! My colleagues on the Arizona team for doing Augmentative & Alternative Communication evals (they each do 2 - 6 evaluations per month), have suggested some iPad apps for supporting attending, tracking, motor planning, plus some communication apps. I'm hoping that a 20-something 'digital native' who is reading this will make a time to meet with Cindy & Diane this week to help download the apps (they have a list) and give them a quick training in use! Thanks!

Di Raborn
November 17, 2011
What David has shown us of late:

He has written his name many times. We have taken a photo of this as he has done this.

He has said the word "Yes" twice; once to me and once to Alana a couple of weeks ago when asked if he was scared they would drop him.
He has said "Amen" to his father~

He wrote: "Hey Aunt Cindy"; "Hey, Mother"
When asked where Aunt Cindy lived he wrote "Rome, GA"~
When asked by the Olympic track athlete, Carline Muir
(Canada 2012) to play the flag-country game, he wrote
Jamaica correctly for gold/green. He wrote "Lima" correctly
when asked to play the capitals game. Ie: What is the capital
of Peru. He beat Carline in two (2) games of tic-tac-toe.

When his brother who is a scientist (Genetics PhD candidate
2011) showed him the 'big ten helmets' on Skype, David
wrote the names of the teams and their team names on the
whiteboard for him: Iowa–Hawkeyes; Indiana-Hoosiers;
Purdue-Boilmakers; Wisconsin-Badgers~etc. all spelled
correctly and legibly~ @broborn nailed all of my #BigTen
Q's, naming the teams represented by my football mini
helmets. David's in there! Love you so much bud!

There is much more. He has manipulated a camera and taken
many pictures of groups of people, framing it and centering
it. He has shown me what to do on the computer by using the
cursor.

He is very weak as it was just discovered that he is low in
cortisol (19 (I think) as opposed to the normal over 100
range).

Sharon Scheirer
November 17, 2011
Praying and hoping with you... and cheering David on!
Gregg and Sharon

Ryan King

November 21, 2011

So great to hear and see how Dave is progressing!! I get really excited to get online every morning and see the updates of the day. Brandon sent me a picture the other day of David's writing and it made me so happy to see him able to communicate with others. I will be landing December 18th in Edmonton and the hospital will be my first stop as soon as I land.. bags in hand.. I cant wait to see you **David Raborn**.. Miss you buddy

Linh Bui Raborn

November 21, 2011 · Iowa City, IA, United States

Hi Dave, a couple of days ago, I dreamt of me going up there, cooking the rice soup with chicken for you, and you told me it's yummy with a big, beautiful smile -> let's make that dream come true together, dear! We're all proud of you!

Tamara Fisher Avery

November 21, 2011 · Sherwood Park

Nathan was proud to be able to bring you his football team's trophy on Friday. We think you deserve a trophy for all of the hard work you are doing everyday. You are amazing!

Katie Musselwhite-Goldsmith

November 21, 2011

Wow Dave! I see that you are writing! And, more legibly than my own writing... I'd like to add! What great news! I'm looking forward to hearing more great news. Ethan slept on his top bunk for the first time last night and requested that his Dino Dave also join him!

Jeff Marchand

November 23, 2011

Buddy just heard you're talking that's amazing news so glad to hear that!!!! Keep going bud let's get you outta that stupid bed and back out there!!

Adam Tuckwood

November 23, 2011

This morning marks a great step for David. During an assessment of Dave's progress while writing answers on a board, David decided, enough of this noise, and spoke. And continued to speak. He answered many questions about his life and his surroundings, and did so with correct answers. In honor of this monumental step, we at beards for bro born (along with the Raborns) have decided its time. It's SHAVE FOR DAVE time. Please send in your pre and post pics to the beards for bro born site, although I haven't asked the two upstanding gentlemen that put that together, I'm sure they will post them all some can see how terrible (actually awesome) we all look. Big day!

Kevin Meleskie

November 23, 2011 · Sherwood Park

Taylor asked Dave what the funniest part of today was and Dave wrote "frank pooped" (his roommate) we all laughed real hard and Dave giggled and smiled. It was amazing to see his big grin again. Love ya buddy Xo

Gray Alton

November 24, 2011

Hey big D! I haven't posted in a while. I will pray for you tomorrow, like I have every day, and when your back up and going strong again I will bring Honey back up to see you again so you can play with her (our dog...not Kate...for everyone else...honey loves Dave). You're a rockstar and we all love you brother! I'll come see you as soon as I can get away from Calgary. "Be strong and courageous. Do not be afraid or terrified because of them, for the LORD your God goes with you; he will never leave you nor forsake you." Deuteronomy 31:6

Taylor Raborn
November 25, 2011 · Edmonton
"Jesse Palmer is so dreamy." - David, telling jokes during the Halftime Show of the Iowa-Nebraska game.

Di Raborn
November 23, 2011
Please pray for Dave's surgery tomorrow. a. that it occurs and b. that it is safe and all goes w/ 150% success rate. Thank you and God Bless.

Taylor Raborn
November 24, 2011 · Edmonton
David just got back to his hospital bed after his surgery about 45 minutes ago. There were no complications and the surgeons took their time and were very thorough. He now has a complete, intact skull and we are all very happy about it.
I will write a full update for the group soon.

Kevin Meleskie

November 24, 2011 · Sherwood Park
Taylor will elaborate I'm sure but for all of you anxiously waiting for news, Dave is out and it apparently went well. Xo

Di Raborn
November 25, 2011
Going to get some shut-eye after Dave's surgery. Confident he will have healing sleep, keep quiet and his head still throughout the night so he can wake refreshed after surgery to replace his 2 bones on his skull. Thank you, Taylor for spelling me!

Curtis Haugan
November 25, 2011
Hey Dave, been following the posts on this group ever since I heard about the accident, and have been praying for a miraculous recovery for you since then. Everything I have been reading seems to indicate that you are experiencing just that! So happy for you and your family, and what an answer to prayer. I hope you receive some healing rest after your surgery, and that you continue to defy the odds with your amazing determination. Much love.

Andrew Obrecht
November 25, 2011 · Calgary
Hey Raborn. It's been a little while since i wrote but there hasn't gone a day that you haven't crossed my mind. I'm really happy to read about your constant improvement. The strength that you are demonstrating to accomplish things that many would not be capable to do is something to be admired. Continuously sending you as much strength and energy as I can. –Obie

Chris Han

November 26, 2011

hey dave i'm driving down from grande prairie today to come visit if you're ready. i always seem to catch you specifically at a time of surgery tho haha. but i would say my presence

signifies major milestones towards your recovery 😃 =P see u soon buddy

Kevin Wuthrich

November 28, 2011

Keep fighting Dave buddy. Love you miss you. We're thinking about you out here. See you soon!

Laura Eva

November 28, 2011

You will make it through this, David. You have proven time and time again how strong you are! Thinking of you and sending positive vibes your way xo

Adam Tuckwood

November 28, 2011

Hello everyone.

This morning it was noticed that David had experienced a bleed over the night. He is currently in an emergency surgery to resolve this. The surgery will involve reopening the skull, but the bone flap should be replaced before he leaves. It is likely that after this surgery he will return to ICU, due to the doctors suspecting he will have to remain intubated after the surgery. The duration of his stay at the ICU will depend on

217

his progress. At this time the Raborns have asked for your prayers. David is in for another fight and will need us there with him. I will update as I hear. Best wishes.

Adam Tuckwood
November 28, 2011
We just heard that David is out of surgery waiting in recovery. He will be brought up to ICU as soon as he's ready. We haven't heard how things went or what was found out as of yet. I will up date as I hear. He is currently going for another surgery to have a type of net in a vein. This is being put in to help to manage the blood. Lot that formed in his leg. The hope is with this net in place they will be able to Wien David off his blood thinners which will help avoid bleeding situations like the one today. He has not returned from that yet, but his family has seen him and it sounds positive. Keep the prayers coming. Best wishes.

Taylor Raborn
November 28, 2011 · Iowa City, IA, United States
Further to Adam's post, David is now out of surgery. A skull bone was replaced and two drains inserted in his head. He is now staying in the ICU for monitoring until further notice. Thank you for your messages of support- I will post when more information becomes available.

Adam Tuckwood
November 28, 2011
Hello everyone.
David's surgeon feels that the surgery went well. He doesn't suspect this should slow David's recovery too much.

218

Candace Miller

November 29, 2011

Good Morning David!!! This is the day that the Lord has made. We shall rejoice! and be glad this day! So excited for good reports on a very long and challenging day yesterday. Blessings on you young man, packed down and running over. Have a fantastic day today.

Adam Tuckwood

November 30, 2011

Hello everyone.

Went to see David this morning, was treated with wide eyes. I spoke with him and let him know everyone was thinking of him and that we were there with him. Spoke with a few of his nurses and learnt he has spoke a little (name and city he is in) and he gave me a pound on my way out. He is still currently in the ICU but the nurses feel he is ready to leave, when a bed becomes available. Keep the support for Dave and his family coming. It is helping them so much. Best wishes.

Taylor Raborn

November 30, 2011

Dear Team David:

It's been a few weeks since my last update, and much has changed regarding David's condition. There have been ups and downs, but I'm happy to report that despite some recent shocks, the ups outnumber the downs, and we can say with

219

certainty that he is much better today than he was earlier this month.

But first let me address David and our family's recent scare, which Adam and I posted about briefly earlier this week. Early Monday morning David's medical team noticed that David's right eye was closed shut, and a physical exam uncovered the cause: blood pooling behind the eye. David was rushed to radiology and given a CT scan, which revealed that he had sustained another hematoma inside his skull. Dr. Chow and the capable neurosurgery team took David into surgery to stop the bleeding and heal the injury. The bleed was identified quickly enough to prevent dangerous levels of pressure on the cerebrum to build up. The surgery was a success and David spent the next two nights in the neuro ICU with round-the-clock nursing care. He was responsive non-verbally on Tuesday, when his anesthesia was removed.

This was obviously a big shock to our family, who had borne witness to several weeks' worth of sustained improvements. The cause for the bleed was clear: on Thursday the two pieces of David's skull that had been removed were surgically repaired (more on this to follow). David's heparin (a blood thinner) treatment was resumed on Sunday evening as a precaution against a clot from his leg (a Deep Vein Thrombosis) entering his lung (a severe condition known as a pulmonary embolism). It was after the standard four-day window usually given after surgeries, but this heparin caused a bleed in the healing area within David's skull. This was set up as a classic treatment dilemma (DVT/PE vs. potential bleed) and no member of our family blames David's medical team for this setback. They acted swiftly and David is no longer in much danger.

To remove David entirely from the clot-busting (and potentially deleterious) effects of heparin, a small filter (a Greenfield Filter) was placed in the inferior portion of David's largest vein, his vena cava. This was performed not with open-heart surgery, but instead by an interventional radiologist using a minimally invasive technique. The filter was placed in a catheter inside David's femoral vein and it was guided all the way up his body and set into place. If, at a future data a part of the clot (DVT) in David's left leg does at some point become dislodged, it will not reach David's lungs but instead will be caught by the filter. The entire process for this procedure, I'm told, took less than 45 minutes.

Needless to say, the past few days were a whirlwind for David and our family. Currently David is in the neuro ICU waiting to return to a room in the neurology ward. His head bandages have been removed along with the drains. He is communicative, but only non-verbally for now. At the moment he is watching some football on a computer. We are hopeful, and his doctors expectant that he will resume his recovery without too much of a hitch.

What should not be lost in all of this is how far David has come over the past few weeks. It's important that I recap this for all of us, so we don't lose track of these truly positive developments.

At the time of my last update David was alert and non-verbally responsive, but his head, neck and limb movements were limited. Last Wednesday morning, David said his first words since the accident. His Speech Language Pathologist and I were in his room and began to play a game that David's Aunt Caroline, a specialist in this area, had expertly suggested. The game was called 'idiom completion' and involved saying common phrases like 'they fought like cats and ___', and 'a chip off the old ___' leaving an expectant pause for David to speak and finish the phrase. Incredibly, he did. This had the effect of overcoming the 'initiation' deficit that he appears to have, priming his pump. After completing a half dozen of these, David began to answer direct questions. He answered all of the questions we asked him, which included naming the Calgary Dino's mascot that adorned his room ('Rex') and showed a small sign of his customary humor. Question: 'Does is snow in July?' David's reply: 'Sometimes', is not only funny but quite prescient given Northern Alberta's erratic climate. It was more moving that I can say to hear David's voice again, and I would be lying if I told you that I never feared that this day might not come. It's softer and more guttural, not the voice that I remember, but I'll gladly take it for now. Between that wonderful Wednesday morning and his skull surgery on Thursday afternoon, David spoke quite a bit- short, few-word replies. The barrier appeared to be the breath required to generate sound- he appears to be relearning how to talk, and using all of the muscles that we take for granted.

Speaking of muscles, David also spent time retraining his last week doing physical therapy. David's PT team, Joanne and Alana, are truly excellent practitioners, and it was a pleasure to work with them as they trained David. During his daily (provided he is not in surgery) sessions in a large training room, David worked on posture exercises, learning to sit up and eventually stand up (with assistance). During the course of each session, David works so hard that by the end his eyes begin to close from exhaustion. On Wednesday night I asked David what his favorite part of the day was, expecting him to say 'talking' but he (too tired to talk) surprised me by writing 'PT'. It was at that point I realized the depths of David's commitment to getting better. He's not going to quit on himself our us as he brings himself back from this horrific injury.

On Thursday afternoon David went in for surgery, returning his two skull bone flaps to his skull and fixing his 'dent'. The swelling in David's brain had been gone for over a month and it was important for safety as well as self-image reasons to go through this procedure. It was a success and David was feeling spry enough on Friday morning to watch his Hawkeyes lose to Nebraska and follow this up with a full physical therapy session. This time David performed additional exercises in which he picked up and stacked colored cones with each hand. Currently his right hand further along than his left, possibly because during the early days after he woke up his left hand was attached to an IV line.

Friday was significant because at the end of the PT session David took his first, small steps. Supported by Joanne and Alana, and with me yelling encouragement, David walked about two meters before all of the color drained from his face and he fainted! Supported by the three of us, he didn't fall but needed to lie down on the table for a few minutes to regain his bearings. This is further evidence that David is willing to go the extra mile to make progress in his therapy. David's work ethic in his PT sessions would inspire even the most cynical and callous soul.

So where are we now? With the return of his speech, David is now out of a coma, a journey that took two months and one day. He has begun the first stages of what is to be a long and comprehensive rehabilitation that will continue at the University of Alberta Hospital and eventually the Glenrose Rehabilitation Hospital in the next few weeks. He will have to relearn how to do all of those tasks we all do so easily, but as David has shown us, he's more than up to the challenge.

How far his progress has been delayed by the recent bleed is unclear, but we all expect David to be talking again by the end of the week. This was certainly an ordeal, but as much as anyone, sometimes I myself need to pan out and view the entirety of the road that David has taken. It's not always a smooth path, but it's pointing in the direction of a more intact, healing David. And less than a week after American Thanksgiving, that's something that I am truly thankful for.

Please keep your support and encouragement for David coming. As a family we are all so grateful for it, as we are you.

With sincere thanks,
Taylor

Di Raborn
December 1, 2011
Thank you for coming to sing to Dave, Dr. Christine! It was wonderful!

Kassandra Lynn Camponi
December 2, 2011

Hey Dave, I was reading this verse the other day and thought of you. "Have I not commanded you? Be strong and courageous. Do not be terrified; do not be discouraged, for the Lord your God will be with you wherever you go." James 1:9. Keep up the great work!

Kassandra Lynn Camponi

December 4, 2011

"So do not fear, for I am with you; do not be dismayed, for I am your God. I will strengthen you and help you; I will uphold you with my righteous right hand." Isaiah 41:10. Keep fighting Dave! We are still praying for you constantly, and our church is praying for you!

Taylor Raborn

December 5, 2011

A quick note: David has been placed in isolation in the neuro ICU after he was found to have an active infection in his GI tract. This explains why David was having difficulty of late absorbing nutrients. I will provide a comprehensive update regarding this once his medical team provides us with a more complete picture.

Taylor Raborn

December 6, 2011

Another quick update: as of this moment David's GI infection appears to be under control after treatment with powerful antibiotics. He remains in strict isolation in the neuroICU. He showed more energy today, which is an excellent sign.

I will compose a comprehensive update for all of you once

our family gets more information on David's status, most likely tomorrow.

-Taylor

Lisa Holowaychuk
December 7, 2011
D ! The Holowaychuk's are praying for you ALWAYS. Wishing you the best, and so grateful to have you in our lives. The joy you have brought us all is something that I can never truly describe. I know that each day you grow stronger, and each day God is healing every cell, vein, bone and muscle fiber in your body... 2012 is going to be a big year ! I am heading home for the holidays in a couple weeks & can't WAIT to see you ! sending love & wishes always. xoxo – L

Colleen D'Something
December 8, 2011
Three times I pleaded with the Lord to take it away from me. But he said to me, "My grace is sufficient for you, for my power is made perfect in weakness."

Therefore I will boast all the more gladly about my weaknesses, so that Christ's power may rest on me. That is why, for Christ's sake, I delight in weaknesses, in insults, in hardships, in persecutions, in difficulties. For when I am weak, then I am strong.- 2 Corinthians 12:8-10, NIV

Adam Tuckwood
December 12, 2011
Hello everyone. Just a few quick things. As many have heard David is now out of ICU and is back on the unit he was prior

to his set back. He is still on isolation at this time but this in no way means he cannot have visitors. He is definitely able to except visitors and I encourage you to go see him if you would like to. I have heard some people have been avoiding worried about his infection and the chances of catching it. So I'm just going to clarify a few things. Like what has been said this bug is a big one and it is contagious BUT with the type of interaction you will be having with David, and proper hand hygiene on your way in and out of his room, your chances of getting it from David are VERY low. The reason for David's isolation on the unit is due more to there being a potential risk for other immunosuppressed people on his unit. The average healthy person often has this bacteria in there system ordinarily, and it is kept in check through normal body function. The reason it became an issue with David was likely due to his body fighting in other ways, and perhaps also due to some of the other medications he had been taking, so this bacteria was able to get to a point where it caused an problem. Hopefully that will put some of the worries to rest, and if you have any questions please feel free to contact me. AND if you have been worried to visit David due to this, worry not my friends (but do wash your hands).

Taylor Raborn
December 12, 2011
Dear Team David:
I wrote a piece about a trip David and I took together late last year, and what I means for me today. I hope you enjoy it if you have time to read it.

Sinatra and Hope
By: Taylor Raborn

As I approach our family's most difficult Christmas I often return in my mind's eye to one of its happiest, which happened to be just a year ago. Provided with the use of our close family friends' condominium in Palm Springs, we were given a rare (and admittedly welcomed) reprieve from the mid-winter chill of Northern Alberta.

Approximately ninety minutes' drive inland from Los Angeles, California's Coachella Valley is a desert oasis of golf courses and hiking trails, resorts and tennis courts. This landscape is surrounded on three sides by striking mountain ranges, the most prominent being the San Jacintos. As we admired the vistas and perhaps also our wise decision to temporarily relocate here, one of us pointed to their snow-flecked peaks and joked that this year's iteration still qualified as a 'White Christmas'. The green and brown-hued desert expanse provided a playground that was as novel as it was rewarding; activities that in Alberta are restricted to more bountiful half of the year now outstretched before us. And while this trip produced many notable memories- daily tennis matches with David, listening to stories recounted to us by our sweet grandmother ('Namma'), Midnight Mass together at a charming Spanish Colonial-style chapel, the 97th Rose Bowl Game in Pasadena - one event stands out today as I reminisce.

Two days before the New Year David and I rented road bikes from a local outfitting service. We had both recently acquired an interest in cycling, and going on a ride together proved certain to fulfill our mutual, incessant desires for exploration and exercise. At mid-morning the bikes were dropped off at the gates of our complex, and after a few minutes of planning

228

and discussing our trip we embarked.

It is often said that today's California was purpose-built for the car, and the Palm Springs area stands as testament to this claim. In an ideal climate for cycling, we found it less than hospitable to bicycles during the first few miles of our journey, weaving more cautiously than we wanted in and out of traffic downtown until we reached the road that was to lead us on a southeastern arc through the many cities dotting the valley. Cathedral City, Rancho Mirage, Palm Desert, Indian Wells, La Quinta and Indio- to us they were more ideas than entities. One was the site of a famous ATP Tennis Tournament, the other hosted a longstanding PGA tour event. They were playgrounds for people whose success we respected but never envied. Bob Hope was said to love this area more than any other, and as we left the city behind and coasted along the ridge toward the heart of the valley, the enveloping views provided the late star's justification.

In an area boasting more than one hundred and twenty golf courses, it remains a mystery to me why David and I never played a single round during our visit. The few times I asked him he would suggest something else, basketball, weightlifting or tennis. I speculate that to David, these carefully manicured golf courses, and perhaps golf itself represented an endpoint one that he hadn't yet reached. One day he'd deserve to golf here, but not now. He had miles to go, a career to settle on, a life to make. David was a striver in the truest sense, and golf in Palm Springs was to be striving's reward. Not now, not yet. Of course this wasn't a completely rational construction: we could have afforded to play a single round without difficulty, but I suspect it provided tinder for the flame burning inside him.

Less than 5 miles into our trip we encountered a sign in front of a local High School advertising a Holiday basketball tournament: enticement enough for us to dismount and lock up our bikes. After purchasing our tickets, we sat down in the half-full bleachers to watch two lower-ranked teams warm up before the Desert Classic's 7th Place Final. The bright squeaks of basketball soles sliding against the gym floor resounded through the building, a welcome sound to those who like basketball. A team from suburban Las Vegas jumped out to a big lead against the hometown Cathedral City Lions, and the two of us began carefully appraising the action like the former players and current weekend warriors we were. During the action, we made comments to each other like: 'He's got to close that out', 'they have no true point guard', 'their bench is fairly thin', both naively confident that we could throw on a tracksuit and direct either of the respective squads. Glancing at my watch, David indicated that we should be moving on, and we walked together out of the gym. A few yards before we reached the exit, I noticed a crumpled green piece of paper on the floor near the sideline. Picking it up, I found that it was a one hundred dollar bill- a 'Benjamin', as David would remark, half-seriously using the worn urban reference.

There was never a thought of pocketing the money. Together we found the nice female teacher who sold us our tickets and handed her the bill, explaining how and where it had been found. Saying our goodbyes, we strolled out into the bright courtyard of the school where our bikes were secured against the gate. I immediately began to sour on my good deed, and expressed this to David. After all, one hundred dollars would pay for a ticket to the Rose Bowl, a game we were planning to attend together in two days' time.

As we unlocked our bikes, David reacted quickly to my sudden change of heart. "Why are you complaining?" he said. "It was the right thing to do. We shouldn't expect a reward for doing what's right."

I begrudgingly agreed with him, slightly surprised by how adamant he sounded. If anyone could appreciate having to pinch pennies, it was David. Only a day prior to this one he had griped about his lack of funds, openly questioning whether attending the Rose Bowl, a game both of us had grown up watching together, would be worth it.
Slightly embarrassed by my abrupt vacillation, and realizing my sudden bout of selfishness, I relented and told him that he was right. As we strapped on our helmets a woman's voice called out to us from the edge of the courtyard.

"The Tournament Director would like to thank both of you for returning the hundred-dollar bill," she said. Surprised at the timing of this reward, we followed her back into the gym and met a large, energetic man, who offered us our pick of any of the shorts displayed on the tables next to the court. Thanking the man for his kindness, we each selected the pair that we preferred. David, after a brief negotiation, left with the only pair that was initially 'off-limits', a white, red and yellow 'McDonald's All-American' pair that I secretly coveted as well. David would sport these shorts for a majority of the days left on the trip.

This was the type of good fortune that I would associate with David during those heady days before the evening of

September 22nd. Doing right was its own reward, but sometimes it was honored with a token of appreciation: in this case, basketball shorts, no small prize for either of us. As we returned to our rented bikes and pedaled away from Cathedral City High School, I couldn't help but smile at his serendipity.

Continuing southeast, we soon entered the city of Rancho Mirage, marking the heart of the desert's golf-resort country. Situated along the palm-lined avenues were some of the most tony courses in the country, boasting names like Tamarsk, Desert Island and The Springs. When we made an inquiry, black iron gates and a security attendant firmly prevented us from satisfying our curiosity of exploring one of these resorts, but we just smiled and continued on our way, secure in our current endeavor and confident that these oases of leisure would open their doors to us at a future date, if we still cared.

Riding across the intersection of Frank Sinatra and Bob Hope Drives, I suddenly pictured the two icons together: the suave crooner and beloved swaggering comic holding court at a canteen somewhere in this valley. The image was indelible, if fantastical. I told David that we had just passed the most charmed address in the world, given the significance of its namesakes and buttressed on all sides by carefully manicured paradises. He agreed, laughing, but I don't think either of us believed it. We were just happy; enjoying our ride and our fellowship, exploring a new place. We didn't need blue skies and ubiquitous palm trees, but on this day they would render externally the aesthetic we felt on those endless yet somehow fleeting days we shared. Sinatra and Hope was wherever we happened to be, together.

The next few hours of our ride were enjoyable but not extremely eventful: a brief detour through a publically accessible resort, a late lunch in Indian Wells, but we soon realized that we were running out of light. We had just over an hour left before darkness would set in. With more speed and urgency we hurried through the adjacent towns. As we headed eastward through La Quinta, the landscape lost its resort-like feel. The street names we crossed did not correspond to the environment: Bliss and Bonita (Spanish for 'lovely') felt like wishful thinking at best, false advertising at worst. We passed empty desert lots, and as we entered Indio even the sidewalks, where we had began to ride due to the narrowing roads, disappeared. This was not the Indio of the Empire Polo Club and Coachella Music festival: this pocket of homes was a grittier, tougher place that was perhaps intentionally tucked away between two large highways, out of sight and out of the minds of vacationers. I suspect that it was here that some of the legions of short-order cooks, busboys and housekeepers that the resort economy demanded were forced to live, unjustly shut out of better housing because of its prohibitive cost or their own immigration status.

It was now nightfall. Acclaimed travel writer Paul Thereux once described the abrupt tropical sunset, and we were both caught off guard by its suddenness. The sun's light did not so much fade as switch off, a celestial light bulb. Now only the scattered light of functioning streetlamps illuminated our path. Aggressive motorists in succession passed us very closely on our left, as if to let us know that we weren't welcome. A youth wearing a black hooded sweatshirt feinted

233

towards us as we rode by, reinforcing the message. The homes lining our route, once modest but well-maintained, became openly dilapidated. Medium-sized, underfed dogs with no resemblance to any current breed roamed the dimly lit, empty cross streets. A particularly fierce dog took off after David's bike, audibly scaring him and biting at his heels before giving up and lurking away into a dark yard.

We were never in true danger, but we were unsettled, and had reason to be. Those roughly thirty minutes seemed to be an eternity. As we crossed the narrow overpass toward our destination David sprinted ahead, giving a mock cheer, unconvincingly disguising his relief. The shopping center was lit up in the evening sky, a suburban beacon that now felt strangely welcoming. Later that evening we would laugh at our self-imposed predicament, but we felt brief and real moments of fear, tempered only by the other's presence. Our father picked us up in his rental car a half hour later and we drove off toward Palm Springs together.

Much like the desert sun that day, the light that once shone brightly in my life has crashed beyond the horizon without warning, and darkness obscures my path. Real, sustained danger, not the fleeting or imagined kind, is now before us. In my internal dialogue, the bike accident that took David from us that September evening is called 'The Darkness', the most appropriate way I know of to describe a Hell that I would wish upon no soul on earth. David's friendship brought me true light and joy, as I wander through life today I summon memories like our ride through the Coachella Valley. They provide just enough light to stay on my path. For an instant, we're at the corner of Sinatra and Hope once again.

As David is confined to a hospital bed, in those unoccupied instants between blood tests and being turned, prodded or adjusted, the independence he so dearly prized stripped away, I like to think that he returns to the many moments we shared together as I do, accessing them like we would a glossy-paged book on a shelf. I hope they provide a glimmer of solace amidst the pain, anguish and confinement, that his memories of us provide the comfort I cannot give him today. Sometimes, in solidarity, I place myself in that bed, experiencing his total frustration and restriction. I lack the courage to stay long; his quiet agony overwhelms my defenses. Instead I pretend that David can leave that cramped, beeping room and the fluorescent corridors, his spirit unrestrained by physiology or gravity. He flits about my world when he's not in Buenos Aires or Budapest, Peterborough or Pasadena, places both known and unknown. I see him a stranger's smile, the knowing kindness of a friend or colleague. He chides me when I miss an open look in basketball, reassures me when life is at its bleakest.

Our Judeo-Christian tradition tells us that darkness cannot overcome the light, flickering stubbornly and unyieldingly somewhere in the endless expense of time and space. My love for David and his spirit live inside me, enveloped by this Darkness that cruelly descended upon our family. Maybe it is his memory that is my Light- a source of strength that proudly resists doubt and fear.

Until we can ride together again I will remember David actively and unceasingly. Memory is power. His perfect jump shot, the way his eyes flashed talking about an idea he developed, his insatiable desire to explore new territory, geographic and metaphorical: they remain as real today as they ever were. The experiences we had, the bonds we forged, the fraternal love- they burn unceasingly inside our souls. This light cannot be extinguished by the Darkness; these memories endure and can never be scrubbed away.

Our bike ride one year ago is in some ways a microcosm of my relationship with David. We set out not truly knowing where we were going, we made frequent detours on our journey, and he taught me important lessons along the way. Darkness set in abruptly, long before we expected, and today we are in unfamiliar and unwelcome territory. Stray dogs chase David, gnashing their teeth. I can offer us no other solution but to keep going. If I look closely I swear I can make out the glow of lights and safety ahead.

Keep pedaling David. Please keep pedaling. I'm right behind you.

Adam Tuckwood
December 15, 2011
Hey everyone. Saw Dave a couple times today. He looks good, his face is filling out again. Did our handshake on my way out the first time, second time he was pretty tired. Pop in and see him of you can I know he'd love it. Best wishes.

Sherry E. Cameron
December 18, 2011
Don't know you all personally, but have been praying for your whole family. We spoke of Christmas miracles in church today and I thought of you Dave. The gift of love and hope of the 659 people that you have brought together in faith is

236

amazing. Each step forward is a miracle that we all are sharing together. I thank you for allowing me to be a part of your prayer team...part of your recovery family and look forward to meeting you one day! Merry Christmas.

Susan Holtby – Davey Holtby's mom
December 21, 2011
Hi! The family doesn't know me but my son was on David's team at the summer NBC camp. We received a post card from David yesterday, obviously written right after camp. It still took me back and gave me pause again to pray for his recovery and strength for his family.

Di Raborn
December 23, 2011
Dave is in surgery right now having a filter taken out of his heart valve. I think it is a routine procedure.

Kevin Meleskie
December 30, 2011 · Jasper
Wish you were here buddy, I'll be thinking of you and toasting to your good health in front of the whole crowd. Love you and I'll be drawing on your strength up there to keep the nerves down. Xo

Di Raborn
December 31, 2011
Happy News Years 2012 to everyone from David and family! Thinking especially of Kevin Meleskie and all the groomsmen @ the JPL this stellar weekend! God Bless you all!

Donna Lafleur

December 31, 2011
Happy New Year to David and family. You may not have physically been at the wedding...but you were sure there in all of our hearts. Love from the Lafleur's.

Taylor Raborn
December 31, 2011
Dear Team David:

As the last moments of 2011 fade away across the world and we look toward a new year, I thought it appropriate to send you all a Holiday greeting from our family as well as update each of you on David's condition.

After rapid progress for David in October and November, December was a difficult month, and it be would misleading for me to say otherwise. We began the month under ominous circumstances, as David underwent a frightening and unexpected bleed (epidural hematoma) on November 28th, four short days after his skull fragments were surgically returned to his head (a cranioplasty). Prior to this event, David had made what remains his furthest progress to date: he was talking consistently, had a relatively high amount of energy and was participating in rigorous physical therapy sessions. On November 23rd, aided by his physical therapists, David took his first few small steps.

I'm afraid that David did not reach those heights again in December, and progress has been unsteady and complicated by other unforeseen medical issues. Early in December David acquired a C. difficile infection, which caused sustained GI tract problems. C difficile is a gram-positive bacteria that is particularly difficult to eradicate with antibiotics because it forms seed-like spores (bacilli) which are not themselves destroyed by the medication. This infection has lasted nearly the entire month, and David is being treated with another two-week course of metronidazole. The infection has caused a noticeable drop in David's energy and attentiveness, which is frustrating for all of us, David especially. The only good thing that has come from David's infection is that he has his own private room, one that he wouldn't otherwise be given. We've embraced this space and have tried to make it as comforting as possible for him. The cards, letters, notes and pictures you have sent him adorn the front wall, and he studies these carefully during his quiet moments. I have no doubt that they provide him a dose of good cheer when he's feeling low.

The other major medical issue David is encountering is his Deep Vein Thrombosis (DVT) in his left leg. To refresh us all, a DVT is a large blood clot that, if untreated, could reach and do damage to his lungs, causing what's known as a Pulmonary Embolism. I wrote earlier that, to prevent this, a filter was placed in his vena cava, which is the major vein leading to his heart and lungs. A procedure on the 22nd of December to retrieve this found a small clot embedded in the filter, so his physician has increased the amount of clot-busting drugs (heparin, warfarin) that are delivered to David so that his clot is removed. In a few weeks' time the radiologist will revisit his filter and remove it if possible.

David, I'm certain, is also experiencing bouts of sadness because of the accident and what it has done. Yesterday he missed standing up at the wedding of a good friend, and on

Christmas, a holiday that is very important to our family, he spent most of the day in the hospital bed. On several occasions I've seen a stray tear in his eye, and I expect that he is doing a lot of thinking about his condition and his current disabilities. This emotional burden may have impeded David's progress recently, but it's impossible to know for sure.

I can tell you that throughout this ordeal, our David has handled himself with courage and poise. Nurses poke and move him every two hours. Technicians arrive every morning to draw vials of blood. Machines beep and buzz around him and even in the early mornings his sleep is interrupted by the yells of patients in the ward, drifting down the hallway into his room. He cannot reliably communicate with those who he loves the most. But through it all he retains his dignity. Rather than recoiling or protesting in some way, he is cooperative at every turn. Every relevant communication to me or his parents indicate that he desperately wants to recover and his efforts reinforce this. David inspires me every day, and I imagine that he is inspirational to many of you as well.

Our family is committed to pulling David through this difficult period and helping him get to the Glenrose Rehabilitation Hospital. The U of A Hospital, which so skillfully put David back together in the hours and days after accident, is obviously less equipped to deal with David's condition as it exists today. He does not have an integrated medical team as such, but rather a variety of doctors that do consults and often do not communicate with one another or with our family. We are working to improve this, and will not

240

be deterred nor will we let our David slip through the cracks. As of this moment David can communicate through writing or using hand signals, but only seldom talks. We are working to bring him out in a variety of ways, but sometimes progress in this area is not linear with brain injury patients. His GI infection seems to be responding to the antibiotic treatment, but it will be another 11 days before we will know if the C. difficile infection is gone. His energy levels and attentiveness have improved during the past two days, so there is some good news moving into the next calendar year.

As the New Year celebrations take place at midnight tonight in Edmonton, I will be holding David's hand in his hospital bed. The next year will be better than this one, and he enters it bolstered by the love of so many.

Our family's message to you is one of true gratitude and awe. Your support, manifested in a myriad of ways, is truly and thoroughly appreciated. I wish I were capable of acknowledging here all of you individually, but please know that each expression of love and concern for David and our family gives us more strength to carry on.
Even though David remains in isolation, we encourage and welcome visitors- all one has to do is put on a yellow gown and gloves to see him. Typically, the best times to come are between 11 and 1 or 3:30 and 6, but if you want to have more information on a given day please do not hesitate to contact me.

We hope each of you had a wonderful Christmas and Holiday season, and hope you're your 2012 is filled with love, health and prosperity. The last quarter of 2011 was cruel to our family, but all of you came through for David and for that we will remain thankful throughout 2012 and beyond.

With my fondest wishes for a Happy New Year, Taylor

Taylor Raborn
January 2, 2012
David spoke to me this morning!
A recap-
Me: How are you feeling Dave?
D: Super good
Me: Where are we going to visit when you get out of this bed? D: Disneyland Me: ... [/Happy beyond belief]
This is great progress.
And you're all invited.

Kassandra Lynn Camponi
January 6, 2012
Hey Dave, just so you know we had our small group pray for you tonight! Lots of people are still praying for you! Keep being strong!

Emily Joyce
January 7, 2012
I had two great visits with Dave while I was in Edmonton Thursday and Friday. On Thursday in particular, he really alert and engaged. We visited for an hour and he gave me a thumbs up afterwards--yesterday, he was a bit more tired, but he'd had a very active day ☺ :) Really great to finally visit. Next time I come up to the city, I have no doubt we'll be able to go for a walk and have a good chat ☺

Taylor Raborn
Dear Team David:

A brief, positive update followed by a call for letters to David. After continued struggles with his C. difficile infection, David has made significant progress these past few days.

On Saturday he spoke more than he had since November 23rd, or perhaps even more. We were able to get a glimpse into his desires and wishes, and he was emphatic on one point in particular: he wants to leave the hospital and 'go home'. No one is sure precisely what the cause of this flurry of speaking, but our family hypothesizes that it is due to the antibiotics finally getting traction on his infection. I'm told that being infected with C. difficile takes a lot out of those infected with it, so perhaps his energy levels were sapped so much that he was rendered unable to talk.

David is still unable to carry on conversations, but he has begun asking questions, which represents progress beyond simply replying to queries. Speech therapy, once it begins, will work on David's initiation of speech.

Physically, David remains weak but is stronger now than he has been since the second bleed on November 28th. His range of motion in his left and right arms are improving, so much so that he was able to put on a hat given to him as a gift on Saturday while he was sitting in the Atrium.

He is working with a talented Physical Therapy team daily, and they are working on his posture, strength and flexibility.

243

He has not yet been able to stand on his own, as he did during the days before the bleed in late November, but his PT team is working with him on a large supportive board to familiarize him with the walking position.

Our family is beginning to have more confidence in David's medical team now. After some wrangling on our part, David now has an Internist (a physican who is trained to deal with David's current medical issues) seeing him nearly every day. This is a large improvement from the prior situation, when David would be 'rounded on' (medical jargon for 'visited') by a Neurosurgery resident. The batch of residents on his service did not appear interested in caring for David, and most never even entered his room or gowned up. We're happy with the doctor David now has, and are very hopeful that his current medical issues will be managed properly so that he can move to the Glenrose Rehab Hospital as soon as possible. David's nurses have been quite good, and David is slowly learning how to (and gaining the strength necessary to) press the buttons on his hospital remote to call for a nurse and turn his lights on and off. This is part of recovering the independence David has lost, and no doubt craves.

If his sudden bout of talking this weekend was any indication, we all are looking to this week to be a big one for David.

And now, I have something to ask of you. Since David remains in isolation, he cannot read this blog regularly, because any device, like his computer or iPad, that goes into his room must stay there. David is able to read, and as such I think it would be an enormous boost for him if we all sent him postcards or letters. Many of you around the world have asked me what you can do to help, and this is one positive

244

thing that we all can do, no matter how far away we live from Edmonton. One thing I worry about is David's morale; it must be so difficult to be isolated in his hospital bed. Whether you find yourself in Sherwood Park or Serbia, let's send David encouraging messages through the mail to show him how much love and support he truly has!

Our Dad moved into his new office directly across 114th Street from the Hospital, and the staff have agreed to sort mail addressed to David, so he'll get the mail promptly. I'll post the mailing address in a separate message so that all of you can see it more easily here on the site.

Your support over the Christmas Holidays and into the New Year has been a beacon for the Raborn family. There is not a shred of doubt in my mind that David will be able to tell you, with his own voice, how dearly he treasures what you've done.

With my enduring thanks,
Taylor

Taylor Raborn
January 9, 2012
Team David is now on Twitter! (or should I say #TeamDavid) We just started a Twitter account so that all of you have another way to engage with David's courageous recovery from this terrible injury.

The account is: @DavidsRecovery.
Please note that this account will in no way detract from or replace anything that we do here on this group.

This Facebook group will remain the comprehensive repository for all things regarding David's Recovery, but the Twitter feed will just be another way to stay connected in real time. Most updates will be made by me, but his father will get access as well.

The tweets (aka updates) on this new account are 'protected' (meaning not public), so simply make a request and I'll give you access.

If you don't use Twitter, no big deal- you're completely covered here on this page.
If you do, give @DavidsRecovery a follow!

Best wishes,
-T

Janne Robinson
January 9, 2012 · Edmonton
Hey Dave,

I am reading a book right now called "Broken Open" its a combination of short stories on how difficult times can help us grow. Its one of those battered, crinkled loved books handed down through a few people and re read by each of them. It focus's on many things... the surface level we live our days on, communicating with others on a daily basis. The "how are you's" and generic Good, Fine, Okays. That are not even emotions we tend to communicate with. The honesty we should bring into our lives..Spent lots of late nights with my nose in the book having profound insights.

In the chapter I read yesterday it was the story of a woman who had multiple sclerosis.. her fight in continuing her career, raising her kids. The part that hit home for me the most was when she shifted her perception.

"In the early stages of accepting my disease I would go into my room to rest as if I was about to face the firing squad. I didnt want to feel the level of exhaustion that kept shooting me down, day after day. I didnt want to face my despair. So I devised little ritutals for myself to ease the transistion from " I must keep going on" to " I must rest and heal".

You've been fighting and healing for a long time, and that must feel frustrating. Im sure your at a point where you just feel like.. I am SO done lying here, and I want to get back out there and just live! I cant imagine the frustration that is probably feeling heavy on your heart. I was sick with bronchitis for one week, and kept impatiently waking up every day wondering when I could get back to my routine.. get back to my 9 am yoga class, my three jobs, go for a walk outside with my roomates pup, I felt impatient about just going and doing my dry cleaning.

Sometimes healing takes longer then we want it too.. and sometimes surrendering your will and your stuborness and just knowing that right now.. you need to rest and heal will bring you some mental clarity or a little bit of releif.. You are exactly where you are meant to be in this moment, and everything will wait until you are done healing and resting. The world will still be here to greet you with wide big open hands. You are moving mountains and peoples hearts every

single day fighting from that bed.
So dave I just wanted to write you today to say- Its okay to
rest and heal. You are where you are meant to be.

Sending you love and light.

Taylor Raborn
January 10, 2012
Last week, right before he went to sleep for the night, I asked
David what European city he would choose to visit once he
was well enough to travel. He said 'Edinburgh', which is a
unique and charming place, befitting a unique and charming
young ma
Our family's ancestry is Scottish, and we often call Scotland
'the Old Country' in conversations.

Here's a photo of Scotland's Royal City from National
Geographic.
One day David and I will visit Edinburgh together and watch
the trains go by, much larger versions of the two lads in the
photo.

Di Raborn
January 12, 2012
Dear Team David: Please pray for the surgical procedure to
go well tomorrow to retrieve the filter in Dave's lower vena
cava. This is the 2nd try. Please pray for 'smooth sailing' in
this surgery as you pray for Dave; guidance for all physicians
involved; and, our Lord to watch over him. Thank you from a
mother's heart~

Taylor Raborn

January 13, 2012

Happy to report that the procedure was a success! The filter was removed without difficulty, and David is now resting back in his hospital bed.

Thanks to all of you for your messages of support for David: we've made it over another hurdle together!

Carol Dansereau

January 16, 2012

Hi Diane, I just want you, David, Wayne ,and Taylor,along with all your family to know that you continue to be in our thoughts and prayers every day. Your strength as a family and the strength and love of David's friends is so wonderful. Please take care of your self. I can not begin to imagine how difficult these months have been, but your love and devotion are such an example to all of us.

Di Raborn

January 24, 2012

I took David outside in his chair. This is the first time he has been outside since 22 September! He told Ann, the charge nurse, that it was "brisk" when asked. He also spoke to Erin and Kayla, his 2 nurses, in sentences today. What smiles on their faces!! Yesterday, he asked about Adam Tuckwood by name twice to his dad. Last week, David asked if he could have bottled water when we were in the gift shop. Clear as day. It stung my heart to have to tell him that he had to consistently swallow first. "I can swallow", he said. "The nurses and docs have to see this", was my reply. I now completely understand the meaning behind: "Guarding my heart"~

Kevin Meleskie

January 25, 2012 · Edmonton

And the oilers game stick goes to Mr. and Mrs. Hughes for $225! Thank you so much! We will be gathering all of the money raised and presenting it to the hospital shortly. Team Broborn wants to thank all of you who bought t-shirts etc, Dave is proud of all of us for getting something positive out of a terrible situation.

Kevin Meleskie

January 25, 2012 · Sherwood Park

I'm proud to announce that team Broborn along with the great work from Tammy Zimmer and the dentistry class at the u of a, have collectively raised $5000 dollars to donate to the U of A neuro ICU unit that saved David Raborn's life. A big thanks to everyone who bought T-shirts, the dents, and my new favorite oiler Ladislav Smid who donated and signed his game stick for auction and wished Dave a speedy recovery. We will be donating it shortly as soon as possible, at David's request he wants to be involved in the donation to show his personal gratitude for all of your support and for the hospital staff.

Thanks everyone, a little bit of good can come out of almost everything.

*Note: this money actually went to the Physiotherapy Department.

Taylor Raborn

February 3, 2012

Team David:

Your response to my call for mail went far beyond my most optimistic expectations. Thank you.
Here are your cards and letters covering the walls of David's hospital room- he read, and know he cherishes, every single one.

Walls matter. Just ask my mom.

Taylor Raborn
February 3, 2012
Dear Team David:

In early February, during the depths of our typically cold, North American winters, the darkest season can feel endless. In the high latitudes of Alberta, the sun's brief daily appearances can torment us, as the greater fraction of the day is covered in darkness. This absence of light can shape our collective mood- frustration and despair may creep into our consciousness. But winter's hold is both impermanent and fleeting: signs all around us, large and small, bear evidence of the coming spring. The winter solstice behind us, the earth's tilt now guides our hemisphere just slightly closer to the sun with each passing day. The accumulation of these changes, nearly imperceptible by themselves, give us a day that is roughly 90 minutes longer than it was on December 21st. On the winter solstice the sun set at 4:15, whereas today it did so at 5:18PM. Light is returning to our lives, and the darkness is receding.

Rebirth and renewal are all around us. On January 23rd, Lunar New Year Celebrations rang out in Asian communities and housewolds worldwide, marking the end of the winter and the beginning of summer. In China, this holiday is known as Chūnjié (春節), literally "Spring Festival". Tết, the iconic festival of the New Year in Vietnam, is also referred to as "Spring Festival": 'Hội xuân'.

Closer to home, there are other tell-tale signs of spring: in a few weeks the first flower blossoms will emerge in Victoria, BC. In three weeks pitchers and catchers will report to

252

baseball Spring Training in locations across Arizona and Florida.

In six weeks' time, the first few species of migratory birds will return to the Northern United States and Canada, signaling the advent of spring.

And in a small hospital room in the corner of the University of Alberta Hospital, our David is getting better.

The signs were small and imperceptible at first, and at the outset of the last month he faced many medical challenges that obscured them even further. He was in continued isolation for a persistent C. difficile infection, which gave him severe gastrointestinal problems and likely some dehydration. A large clot in his leg presented a clear and present danger to his health, held back only by the dual therapies of a filter submerged inside his largest vein and continual doses of blood thinners given intravenously. During this dark period, days went by without David talking. Weakened by illness and months of immobility, he could scarcely move his arms more than a few inches at a time.

But even at this nadir, David's spirit remained unbroken. On several occasions I caught the unmistakable glint in his eye, and I knew. When he was doing an exercise passing his mother a ball, she asked him to give it to me. He moved the ball toward my awaiting hand, and I put my hand around it, expecting him to let go. He looked at me, daring me to take it from him. I pulled back, but he refused to let go of the ball. His once taut arm muscle resisted with surprising strength, and his grip on the object remained. A small smile seemed to form on his lips, as if to say: 'this hasn't licked me yet'. In the days before I returned to University, this 'grip game' was a common routine, replacing basketball or tennis as our outlet for competitive energies.

January saw the beginning of what I'll call David's Spring, and during the month he overcame several of the hurdles placed in front of him. His clot receded, then apparently disappeared: his levels of clotting have returned to normal, so his heparin regimen was terminated. For the first time since the accident, David has no IVs entering his bloodstream.

David resumed talking in fits and starts: some days he would talk a great deal, followed by a day with little to no responses. This oscillation is common, especially since David has had to relearn how to do tasks critical for the mechanics of swallowing that for us are involuntary and automatic.

His strength, especially during the past 10 days, has grown immensely, thanks in large part to Joanne and Alana, his dedicated Physical Therapists. They kept his muscles as limber as possible during the sedentary month of December and who push him fiercely but lovingly. On Thursday afternoon, using a rail support, David stood up for the first time since November. The process was slow, excruciating and exhausting, but David didn't quit.

During the past month, David has been seen by an excellent physician, Dr. Hamadeh, who sees him every day. We are grateful to have him, and he is working on making David's eventual transition to the Glenrose Rehabilitation Hospital happen as expeditiously as possible.

Another important milestone was reached today when David was found, after nearly 7 weeks, to be clear of his C. difficile infection. He is now out of isolation but will remain in the same room, which was thoroughly sterilized by hospital staff this evening. While he was able to receive visitors while he was in isolation, there are fewer barriers going forward, and no gloves or gowns will be necessary.

David's neurological signs are all moving in the right direction: his speech is improving, and he is providing longer and more complex answers to questions, and is even asking questions and making unprompted requests, which is a very positive development. Today he asked his mother if he could go home, even for a day. She replied that this is not possible now, but it is truly a day we all look forward to.

David often asks his parents, on his increasingly long trips in his wheelchair through the main floor of the hospital, for a bottle of water. He misses the refreshment and sensation of drinking and eating, and this is still a barrier to overcome: at present all of his nutrition comes through a feeding tube that is inserted into his stomach. As David improves his swallowing he will be given small amounts of water to drink as a test.

What's more, David visibly looks better. His eyes are no longer sunken, his face has color, and his hair is growing over the one hundred and thirty stitches in his head, making them nearly invisible.

An often-cited proverb states that the night is darkest just before the dawn. In time, it seems possible that we will reflect back on the beginning of January at this bleak moment of David's recovery, the deep chill before the long, inevitable thaw.

During this dark month it was your collective love that helped immeasurably. My appeal for letters to David was an overwhelming success thanks to you: he receives mail every day, holding and reading every item that arrives. The barrage of mail has truly lifted his spirits, and they adorn the wall of his hospital bed. I look forward to the hour that he can thank you himself for this great collective show of support, but in the meantime our family wants to say thank you: you are a vital, and dearly valued part of David's fight.

Let's band together and encourage David anew, that February will usher in even more progress in this 'David's Spring'!

With my sincere gratitude,
Taylor

Taylor Raborn
February 17, 2012
Dear Team David:
A quick note, and another appeal to all of you.
David continues his streak of improvement- we are so thankful for this.
Every morning he wakes up early and asks to be put in a new wheelchair, where he waits for his parents to arrive and work with him.

He is stronger in every way, and is now able to keep his head up without support for long stretches of time. He has an increased range of motion, as well as strength, in both arms. I

256

will compile all of his recent successes in an update that I'll pen shortly. As our mother wrote, he was accepted into the Glenrose Rehabilitation Center, and remains at the U of A Hospital until a bed opens up there. (Why the richest province in Canada sorely lacks sufficient space in one of their major rehab facilities is a question that we can all ask our elected representatives)

My appeal to all of you relates to mail.

This coming Monday, February 20th, David will celebrate his 26th birthday at the U of A Hospital. I will arrive to visit him on the 22nd extending next week to 'David's Birthday Week'. I ask that, if you're able, to mail David a birthday card or letter. He truly loves the letters you sent him over the past month, and is able to read them out loud to his father. Letters can go to the same address, which I'll repost above. Improved morale is a big part of David's recovery, and we have you to thank for showering him with love and support.

Let's show David how proud we are of him by wishing him a happy birthday!

With my gratitude,
Taylor

Taylor Raborn
February 18, 2012
Dear Team David:
Yesterday afternoon we received great, unexpected news: David will move to the Glenrose Rehabilitation Hospital on Tuesday!

Mail can still be addressed to his father's office at the U of A; I'll let all of you know if he can receive mail at the new facility. This is a really important milestone in David's recovery and one that you as a group have hastened with your incredible love and support of David during these difficult times.

David is very excited to move to the Glenrose and work on his rehabilitation full-time- this news comes as an early birthday present for him.

With my thanks,
Taylor

Taylor Raborn
February 20, 2012
On February 20th, 1986, a cold, snowy evening in Edmonton, my brother David was born, an event that changed our family forever. I was overjoyed at the impending arrival of a lifelong buddy, one who I could throw the baseball to while our father was at work and would patrol the acres of marshy boreal forests that surrounded our acreage home southeast of Edmonton.

Lifted up by my father, I craned my head toward the nursery room for my first glimpse at this eight pound, four ounce gift, and when he didn't cry after being administered his first shampoo, I exclaimed 'what a brave brother!' for everyone to hear.

David spent the first day of his first year less than 50 meters and two floors away from his current bed at the University of

258

Alberta Hospital, where he'll spend the first day of his 27th year. I would like nothing better than to be by his side on his birthday, but professional commitments will mean that I will arrive in two days.

There are many ways to wish someone Happy Birthday, including numerous songs penned for the occasion. Because of a recent foray into learning the Spanish language, I can think of none better than the traditional Mexican song "Las mañanitas", which translates as "The little mornings". Both its bittersweet melody and profound lyrics make it unforgettable. The song is very fitting for David, who after nearly 5 months in the hospital, is beginning to return to us.

The song opens with the song's narrator reminding the song's recipient that this morning is a new day, just as King David sang about in his Psalms.
Estas son las mañanitas, que cantaba el Rey David

The song continues:
Hoy por ser día de tu santo, te las cantamos a ti
Because today is your Saint's Day (an important holiday in Catholic countries; also a historical naming convention), the narrator explains, we are going to sing for you.
The narrator then sweetly appeals to the recipient to wake up and to see that the dawn has already broken:

Despierta mi bien despierta mira que ya amaneció.
It's a beautiful morning, and the singer describes the scene for the recipient: the little songbirds outside are already singing, and the moon has set.
Ya los pajaritos cantan, la luna ya se metió

The singer then notes his or her happiness at sharing this special day with the recipient. How beautiful is this morning that I come to greet you!
Que linda está la mañana en que vengo a saludarte.

We all come with joy and pleasure to greet you, the singer tells the recipient:
Venimos todos con gusto y placer a felicitarte

The singer then fondly recalls the day the beloved was born. On that day (s)he explains, the every flower bloomed, and the nightingales sang from your baptismal font:
El día en que tu naciste nacieron todas las flores
y en la pila del bautismo cantaron los ruiseñores
The singer reminds the recipient of the dawn that has come:
Sunrise is here; the day has already given us the light of morning.
Ya viene amaneciendo. Ya la luz del día nos dio.

Some versions of the song end in an appeal from the singer to the beloved:
Levántate de mañana. Mira que ya amaneció.
Arise for the morning- see that the dawn is already here.

Las mañanitas is truly fitting for this occasion- not just for David's birthday, but because it comes at a time of David's steady reëmergence into the world. Just as he was born 26 years ago to the day, so too is he being reborn before our eyes.
There were no flowers on the wintery plain of Northern Alberta that cold February evening. The grayscale landscape

was devoid of vegetation. But David's birth brought us more fragrance and more beauty than the blooming of a thousand blossoms.

If there were no birds singing at David's christening, his life that began that day brought us an even sweeter tune. His song, nearly lost to the world, remains, and it now grows stronger every day.

The moon has set on the long dark night of David's injury, which gives way at long last to a new dawn. The sun rises on David, who in turn illuminates us with his words, his smile and his incredible personality.

David's rebirth will continue tomorrow at the Glenrose Rehabilitation Hospital, where he will learn to stand on his own, take his first unaided steps, hone his speech and learn to eat and drink. The milestones stand before him, but they are closer than they've ever been, and David faces them, proud and dauntless.

David's improved speech means his consciousness is becomes accessible to us: this new dawn is also David's Awakening. If it has fallen to me to carry the trumpet to play his song, I fondly look to the day that he can play it for us own his own.

So, dear friends, as we wish David a Happy Birthday, honoring the gift that his life brings us, let us sing to him the refrain of the lovely Mexican tune:
"Despierta mi David despierta mira que ya amaneció."
Wake up, my David, wake up, see that the dawn is here!

And although I'm much older and less spontaneous than I

was 26 years ago to the day, I'm still going to shout "What a brave brother!", because he is just that.

Proudly David's brother,
Yours,
Taylor

Taylor Raborn
February 20, 2012
Dear Team David:

Today is David's 26th Birthday, and his last day at the U of Alberta Hospital.
In three short weeks he has made so much progress: he is stronger in every way. We are beginning to see emotion on his face, including the tears of joy he shed after being told he was accepted into the Glenrose Rehabilitation Centre.

His distinctive smile now creeps onto his lips, reminding us that the David we remember from before September 22nd is returning.

Yesterday a few of David's friends stopped by the Hospital to celebrate his birthday, and he received gifts, talked with his friends, and even played a game of poker. When Gray Alton won the game and took all of the chips, David heartily booed him. That's our David!

I'll have more to say about David's birthday later today, but I wanted to share with you a first for this group- a current photo of David. He has given me his permission to share this photo with all of you.

In this photo he is blowing a noisemaker as he poses with the crew visiting him yesterday for his birthday. It's a whimsical pose of the sort we can imagine him making before the horrible day in September. It's David's distinctive way of telling us that it's still him inside, and that he's returning to us.

Happy Birthday David. We love you. I love you. I'm so proud to call you my brother.
Taylor

My 26th birthday in the hospital.

Taylor Raborn
February 28, 2012
Dear Team David:

A very quick and exciting update.

As I write this, David is eating his first meal in more than 5 months, because he passed his swallowing test yesterday.

On the menu:

Turkey loaf, mashed potatoes with gravy, carrots, peaches and thickened beverages.
I'll bet it tastes heavenly!

He is making rapid progress in every area in his short time and the Glenrose, while I'll summarize for you soon.

What a wonderful day!

Best wishes,
Taylor

Taylor Raborn
February 28, 2012
Dear Team David:

Now that David is settled in at the Glenrose, many of you have asked me how and where to visit him and how to send him mail.

Because the Glenrose keeps David busy with various rehabilitation activities during the normal working day, David has requested that visitors come between 5 and 7PM Monday to Saturday. He's very encouraged by the support you've given him, and treasures the cards and letters he's gotten from you over the past 6 weeks.

For these reasons, I put together an information sheet that provides the address of the Glenrose, directions to David's unit. I also included a map and other pertinent information, including David's new mailing address (the old one is fine too, but this address will get mail delivered directly to him in his room at the Glenrose). Even if you live in Edmonton, consider mailing him a card to show your support. He reads each one carefully and arranges it carefully on the wall in his room.

Your collective outpouring of love, encouragement and support over the past 5 months is one of David's most powerful sources of inspiration. We are so grateful for each of you.

Toward David's continued recovery,
Taylor

Taylor Raborn
March 12, 2012
Dear Team David:

I hope this update finds you all well.

We are entering the first weeks of Spring, and our David is

getting better.

Over two weeks ago, David moved from the University of Alberta Hospital to the Glenrose Rehabilitation Hospital, and since that time his rise has been nothing short of meteoric. For the unfamiliar, the Glenrose Hospital is a large, 244 bed facility adjacent to the Royal Alexandra Hospital just north of downtown Edmonton. It specializes in all aspects of rehab medicine, including treatment of head injuries like that one David sustained. Having stayed with him there during the days after his move, I can tell you that David is receiving exceptional care around the clock. The devotion of the nurses, doctors, support staff and therapists has been nothing but extraordinary, and they take pains to ensure that our family is included is all aspects of David's care. Many of you have already visited him, but for those who have not been in the hospital yet, his room is large, and it has a window that overlooks an atrium within the Glenrose West section of the hospital.

To me, David's rapid ascent these past 6 weeks resembles that of the Prairie Crocus flower. During March, this little plant pushes upwards through the snow, sending forth notice of Spring's arrival despite the still-chilly temperatures.

So many events bear evidence of this. A few days after David moved into the Glenrose, David's physical therapists challenged him to use a walker they had set up to see if he could use it to move around the facility. Although he had scarcely been able to sit up without assistance, let alone stand, David told his therapists that he wanted to try it. Once he was in place, shaky but unbowed, his now frail legs started pushing his feet forward and back in a natural gait: David

266

was walking! He looked up at me as I cheered him on, and the look in his eyes were of a singular determination; the same ferocity in a man who I had watched hoist 80 pound dumbbells to do shoulder presses only months before. In three repetitions, David walked nearly 120 meters through the winding corridors of the Glenrose. When he finished, he told me that his thin leg muscles could simply do no more. But during the next session he was back at it, fiercely committed to beating his previous distance. Please don't ever doubt that David is fighting every second and that he desperately wants to return to us.

This past Tuesday, David ate solid food and drank liquids for the first time in over 5 months. Prior to that, every calorie he consumed was delivered to his stomach thrice daily through a plastic tube in the form of a brown/yellow liquid. After passing a swallowing test the previous day, David was elated to resume eating again. Even though his first meal was a dish of minced meat and mushy vegetables, David could not get enough. Currently his only limitations are water and bread, but another swallowing test this week will determine whether he is capable of consuming these also.

Having lost over 30 pounds from his once muscular frame and expending a great deal of energy with his rehab, David has shown an enormous appetite. Some days he even eats two trays of food for dinner, depending on how rigorous his schedule was that day.

Currently David can sit up on his own, stand up with nearly no support, and his daily trips with the walker become longer every day. He is now gaining enough arm strength to push himself in his wheelchair, something that was unimaginable even weeks ago.

One common denominator amidst this ordeal has been your unyielding support, and the wall of David's room at the Glenrose, which is adorned with your cards, letters and messages, serves as a constant reminder of this. As a scientist I am concerned during my daily work with empirical things: that which can be counted and measured in some way, and calculating a quantifiable relationship to a specific outcome. I can do no such thing with the love and support that you shower on David, now more than 5 months after that dreadful evening in September. There is no scientific meter capable of assaying the hope and inspiration that each of your letters or visits give him. But I have seen firsthand the flash in David's eyes as he reads a thoughtful letter from a friend living 1000km away, and I have seen the quiet pride he carries himself with when he knows that his friends will be visiting him later in a day. Therefore, to me there is no doubt that you make a significant contribution to David's Recovery. Knowing he has a community of friends that support him buttresses his resolve and helps him carry through. Thank you. Truly.

Watching David's struggle so valiantly during his recovery has caused me to think about what it really means to have courage. Undoubtedly the fireman who dashes into a burning building and the bystander who plunges into an icy lake to save a child are both canonical and enviable examples of bravery.

With these thoughts in mind, I fell asleep one afternoon

watching college basketball last month. I awoke unexpectedly to an advertisement for the Florida State University, a well-known land grant institution in Tallahassee where our father went to graduate school. Their mascot is the Seminole, a Native American tribe whose ancestry also includes the blood of escaped slaves and Creoles. Historically, the Seminole Tribe is notable for, among other things, their ferocity in battle and for being the only tribe that never signed a peace treaty with the United States Government. As the narrator intoned, the statue of a Seminole Warrior (whose tribe gives legal assent to FSU for the use of their likeness) riding a horse in front of the football stadium flashed on the screen, along with the word "Unconquered". And although David and my ancestors, early pioneers to north Florida, often found themselves at odds with warring Seminole bands, I could think of no better way to describe David.

No, he is not a warrior in the original sense, dashing over a trench or hurtling headlong into gunfire on a horse or in a tank. There will be no medals pinned on his chest when the battle is over.

His fight is a different. Having been met with one of the worst blows life can hurl at him, David's is a quiet, constant struggle. It is the bravery of learning to stand again when he once burst through grown men on the playing field, the pain of trying to form the same words that once flowed effortlessly from his lips. His day is suffused with the twinge of sorrow that comes with seeing his atrophied form in the mirror in the place where a strong young man once appeared. It is overcoming the frustration that comes with confinement, holding fast when the night is dark and sheer loneliness and fear threaten his inner thoughts.

David cannot escape his burden, but his bears it every day with a courage that, to me, rivals even that of that Seminole warrior elegized in bronze. He seeks our love, but not our pity. Left along the side of a country road 5 month ago, his inner spirit was never broken despite that evening's cruel fate.

Dear friends, our David is Unconquered. I ask that whenever your daily thoughts turn to him, you think of his tenacity, his Will and desire to return to us one day soon. And as surely as the crocus blooms across Alberta's plains this spring, David WILL return.

With my unending gratitude,
Taylor

Taylor Raborn
March 12, 2012
Dear Team David:

It's that time of year again! Growing up in the Raborn household, the month of March was always special, and not because it began with my birthday.

It's the time of year for the NCAA Men's Basketball Tournament, a 64-team (now 68) tournament that lasts two and a half weeks and whose winner is crowned the National Champion. As many of you know, our Dad was previously a professor at and our mom is an alumna of the University of

North Carolina, which boasts one of the most famous and successful college basketball programs in history, producing players like James Worthy and a guy named Michael Jordan. Every Spring, our family would live and die by the progress of the North Carolina Tarheels in the tournament.

I know that many of you follow this tournament, and some even fill out brackets to predict the winners of the tournament games. With this in mind, I asked David if it would be okay with him if we had a Team David Bracket Challenge, with most of the money going towards purchasing something nice for his unit (like a recliner) at the Glenrose Rehabilitation Hospital that will be delivered by David himself. Of course, the entrant with the winning bracket will receive a nice prize (to be determined based on the number of participants).

The rules of the contest are quite straightforward: pick the team that you think will win each game, all the way up to the National Champion. Points are assigned for picking the winner of each rounds' game, with each subsequent round being worth more, all the way up to selecting the champion.

To make this easier for the uninitiated, each team in each of the four regions (East, West, South and Midwest) is seeded from 16 to 1, a '1 seed' being the strongest team, a '16 seed' thought to be the weakest. If you haven't been following college basketball this year (or ever) don't worry: this is certainly not a disadvantage, and often those without prior knowledge of basketball do better than those who do. It's always useful to find out more information about each team using a Google search. A team that peaks at the right time usually makes a deep run in the tournament (see UConn, 2011).

David and I have always loved filling out our brackets, and David is excited for as many of you who are interested to take part in this.

So with that I invite all of you to join Team David's Bracket Challenge!

The tournament seeds were assigned last night, and the games will begin on Thursday morning. The entry fee will be $10, which can be given to David's mom in person, or mailed to David's room. (You can enter as many brackets as you wish) Alternatively, you can send me an email money transfer at taylor.raborn@gmail.com (Canadian Banks). I am setting up a Paypal account for those in the United States and elsewhere.

Although I always like to fill in the winners by hand on a printed bracket, we will be conducting this contest entirely online using CBS's website.

To begin, simply click on the following link to create an account and begin picking:
http://teamdavid12.mayhem.cbssports.com/e
The password is: david2012

Please also feel free to invite your family, friends and coworkers who may not be part of this group. We want this contest to be as inclusive and big (and therefore exciting) as possible, which in turn will benefit the Glenrose Rehabilitation Hospital for years to come. If any of these people do not have access to the internet, let me know and I will email you a bracket to give to them- we can fill in their hand-picks using the site quite easily.

Once all of the members have joined, I will be specific about the prize the winner will get and the gift to be donated to the Glenrose.

Selections will be due before noon Eastern Time (10AM Alberta time) on Thursday, March 15th, when the games begin.

On behalf of David and I, happy Bracket Picking!

Best wishes,
Taylor
Taylor Raborn
March 31, 2012
Dear Team David:

Today, on short notice, David was given permission by his doctors to leave the Glenrose on a day pass and return home to Sherwood Park. He is currently having a great time at home and is watching the Final Four games with his parents.

Since I can't be there for this historic event, below are some words of reflection that I hope shed some light on the magnitude of David's journey, and your centrality in his recovery.

Sincerely,
Taylor

Homecoming

Our David left his house at about 6:15 on a beautiful, bright
fall evening in September. It was Thursday the 22nd, and he
was going to ride his bike, likely experiencing the last gasp of
Autumn before the biting Alberta winter began to take hold.
Petting his dog Pokey and strapping on his helmet, he glided
down our long driveway with a carefree cockiness like he
always did. He had sent me pictures of the countryside as he
headed south, away from Sherwood Park and toward the
forests and pastures of rural Strathcona County. Life was
good and David was happy- excited at the prospects of his
new job, enchanted by a web-startup idea that he was
feverishly but delightedly working on with a group of friends
in the Tech Community. Staying with him at the beginning of
the month at a dear friend's wedding, I had never seen him
like this- captivated and intense, his mind like a high-
performance engine with its governor suddenly released.
Fearless and jaunty, he had caught his stride. With his talents
and charm, the world laid out for David like the late
September harvest he would glide by that evening.

I often trace the route David took that evening in my mind's
eye, the rolling, forested hills and rural sub-divisions that he
passed along the way. They were so familiar to our family
that the roads and the scenery often blended together, in the
process becoming indistinctive. It was along these roads that
David was first driven to hockey practice at age 6. Once- he
was nearly too young to remember- we had lived in another
house, further south, before our father's job took us across
the continent. I would later drive these roads, first online,
using mapping software, then at Christmas, coming home late

274

for dinner from the hospital to try to understand. The leaves were gone then, the poplar forests now bare and skeletal. This Christmas didn't deserve the beauty of snow cover- everything would be dreary hues of brown.

I still don't know precisely which hill David was speeding down when it happened, the gleeful ride and brazen skip over a pothole, a vestigial expression of boyhood and the anticipation of a happiness that he sensed was on its way. He had it figured out- the complex demands of manhood and the marketplace. He could see the future's promise, excited for what was in store.

The wheel struck in the gouge in the road, falling off the bike. The fork hit the unforgiving asphalt catapulting David headfirst into the earth. It would be another 190 days before he would return home.

Literature and history provide us with many tales of homecoming, the most often cited perhaps being Homer's epic 'Ulysses'. After leaving home, the star-crossed Greek would not return to Ithaca for another twenty years- the first ten fighting the Trojans, and the second traversing the Mediterranean at the whims of Fortune. Ulysees fought a giant, avoided capture by cruel temptresses, and navigated his ship past a six-headed monster. David's journey has been far less fantastical but is metaphysically more dramatic. With each passing week he regains a function once lost by his terrible injury, and he fights the demons that invariably haunt when it's dark and still and there's no one around to comfort him. His scenery lacks the glamour of blue water and jagged cliffs; sterilized linoleum and whitewashed walls are the general backdrop of his hospital setting.

This Thursday David's medical team and our family met to talk about David's status. Each of them praised David's work ethic and positive demeanor, and recounted their amazement at his rapid progress since he arrived at the Glenrose 5 weeks ago. They also gave him permission to return home on a day pass the following Saturday after his physical therapy session.

This morning at about 11:45 David returned home, making the 21km trip after gingerly getting into the car, a task he had practiced repeatedly on Friday during occupational therapy. Unlike Ulysses' Argos, his dear dog was not waiting on the porch to greet him; Pokey had died of old age the previous November. The motion of the vehicle regrettably caused him to become sick all over himself on the drive over. But, to me, there will never be a more poignant return home than this one. It was only the skill of his neurosurgeon that fateful night that prevented him dying on the operating table. In early October his organ systems nearly failed, as the profundity of the brain injury sent his core homeostatic processes haywire. Beset by atrophy and infection, before February he was so weak that he could scarcely lift his head for extended periods, and spoke only brief, one or two word responses. He can now talk without difficulty and is able to walk unaided for up to 200 meters at a time.

David will spend the day at home with his family, visiting and relaxing to the backdrop of the Final Four semifinal games, returning at 10PM to his room at the Glenrose. A semblance of normalcy is returning to his life, just as his frame regains the weight and strength that the injury stole away so entirely. In some ways, David is more fortunate than the Greek hero Ulysees. Rather than face opportunistic challengers to home and hearth as Ulysees did, David returns to a united front of friends, family and well-wishers. The odyssey back to Ithaca cost the lives of all of Ulysees' crewmates, while David, during his journey has only gained supporters. You are his crew, and you have pulled the oars with him every one of those 190 days.

The day will come that David will return home for good, and it is my fondest wish for him that our family home in Sherwood Park will only be his address temporarily, before he moves out, and begins his life anew.

On that sweet day, when he does return from the hospital- never to return- it will be your happy silhouettes that will line the driveway, regardless of your physical location. Whether you're in Boston or Beirut, Coralville or Calgary, you provide the inspiration that drives him forward when no one is watching and everything is just so difficult and his wispy muscles shriek with pain. You are why he has never once surrendered, refusing to relent to Despair's Siren Song.

Yes, David is more fortunate than Ulysees, but his journey has not ended.

Let's see him though the final distance, together: Home at last!

Brett Mador
March 14, 2012 · Cranbrook, BC

Dave, I am legitimately worried about the effect of March Madness on your rehab. Even at the best of times, I don't think either of us would leave the TV to get exercise. The professional in me thinks this is a problem, but the real-life me is very excited to share another March Mayhem with one of the only people who understands my yearly obsession.

You've been one of my top NCAA experts over the years. I remember in 2009 when we watched UNC take down Blake Griffin's Sooners then dismantle Tom Izzo & Michigan St. for the championship. Also, the epic bracket poster you made in 2008. I'm expecting another epic March, though I worry about a UNC team with a few key losses and a very tough region (though still having one of the top 2 rosters in the field).

Be seeing you in the bracket challenge. I'd like to say something smug here, but we both know my bracket will be busted by Friday (Saturday if I'm lucky). Enjoy the weekend. I'll be thinking Raborn every time the Heels get a rebound, which is about 50 times a game.

For everyone else: join the Team David bracket challenge! Details are in an earlier post by Taylor. Trust me, the less you know about basketball, the better your chances of winning.

Brett Mador
April 3, 2012 · Vancouver, BC
Great March Madness everyone! This was an especially meaningful March for me because so much of it reminded me of David, his struggle, and all the epic March's we spent together in the past. Most notable was UNC's victory in the

finals in 2009. I watched the game at Dave's place in Calgary. The game was terrible, one of the worst championships ever...unless of course, you are a die-hard UNC fan, since the Tar Heels destroyed the Spartans. I remember distinctly how Dave wouldn't let me go home early despite the lopsided score, citing the perennial "one shining moment" montage that follows the final game as the reason.

And as I heard of Dave's unscheduled day pass home, I wished I could have been there, standing in his driveway in Executive Estates, holding an old school ghetto-blaster above my head playing "ONE SHINING MOMENT".

Dave, you rock. Keep it up. You'll be home for good soon enough. And on the day of your true homecoming, look for me at the end of the driveway. I'll be the guy with the music

Taylor Raborn
April 8, 2012
Dear Team David:

Happy Easter from our family to you and yours!

Last night David spent his first night at home since the accident, and today he attended Easter Sunday service with his family at Bethel Lutheran in Sherwood Park.

He walked down to the altar by himself to receive communion and was greeted before and after the service by many friends and well-wishers.

We are so grateful for all of your incredible expressions of support, and for the numerous prayers, messages, visits, gifts and favours. You all have made vital contributions to David's recovery. We celebrate a far happier Easter today than we did Christmas a few short months ago. We can never say this often enough, or with the sufficient language, but Thank You. With gratitude, Taylor

Taylor Raborn
April 20, 2012
Dear Team David:

Last night I read a short piece at Prairie Lights Bookstore as part of a conference (called 'The Examined Life"; http://www.medicine.uiowa.edu/theexaminedlife/) for Writing in Medicine that is currently going on in Iowa City.

This essay is a retrospective memoir of my experience during the much darker days in late December of last year, before David's spectacular recovery had truly begun.
This is a new piece, and the first work that I'd shared beyond the group. Since you're in many ways a main motivation for my writing, and my favorite audience, I thought I'd share it with you also here today- I hope you enjoy it.

Our David is getting so much better- he's going home tonight for the entire weekend and is gaining strength every day. I am in the process of putting together another video that illustrates his progress for you.

Thank you all so much for your continued support for David. We are close to reaching the point in his recovery where he will be able to communicate with the group directly, but in the meantime we are asking him to focus on his rehabilitation.

Gratefully,
Taylor

Rounds and Remembering

I was abruptly awakened from an early morning haze as a young woman entered my brother's hospital room. Since the night of September 22nd my family had held near constant vigil at David's bedside, after a catastrophic head injury nearly took his life and left him in a coma. My heart was broken, and it was three days after Christmas morning. Not the usual vivid, white landscape of Northern Alberta, but a brown interloper and fitting emblem of the unnatural injustice of my dear David's suffering. Time now lacked its regular periodicity- the grotesque enormity of David's traumatic brain injury bending the fabric of my existence like a collapsed star of a distant universe. Every event before and after slid toward the horror of this new reality.
My closest friend now lay still in an antiseptic room in a forgotten corner of a giant hospital, his explosive body that once rocketed across the gridiron was rotted away, the remaining flesh hung thin on his frame, soft like a package of bagged milk. The most gregarious, likable person I've ever known could barely speak, and the diaper whose outline was visible outside his generic hospital gown cruelly reminded me of his helplessness. Dull nausea was a stray thought away, but I would do my duty and be strong for him, whatever that meant. If holding his hand through the night could give him

comfort, then I would make my fatigue his monument. Through his big blue eyes he spoke verses of fear, confinement and pain, but it was him inside- I knew it- a filial verification deriving from biology but beyond empirical investigation.

Those happy semesters I spent across the country on the stately campus of Queen's University now fueled the slow-burning dread that was a step away. The neuro-anatomy labs recalled the lessons of lesions to the brain cortex. Was the injury to his frontal lobe, irrevocably altering his personality? Did the brain inflammation after the injury wipe away his ability to speak? The cell biology courses now haunted me as I pondered the injury. Did the inevitable cell death from this stew of toxins: 'necrosis' destroy the neurons and axons that formed his memories of himself, of us? Would he remember those endless northern summer nights behind the high school when we honed our craft, me a quarterback and he the receiver -my receiver- four years younger but always the only person I would ever throw the ball to if it was third and long and my life was on the line.

Would he remember our dashing escape from an Elk in Jasper National Park, his first love in Calgary, talking me through my darkest periods, the tender touch of his mother and the intricate trips we'd planned to embark on When? When. What remained, and what could be salvaged? His life was an intricate work of art, could it truly be Him without every part whose sum didn't measure to the whole?

And what of his fear? Was his accident, a fall on a road bike alone on a bright fall evening, his sentence to a life of barriers

282

and separation? Where did he go when we couldn't hold his hand? Was it a place where monsters gnash their teeth, the venom of his newfound Circumstance personified? He must be so scared. Did he remember?

Dreams became my only solace. Once I overslept my alarm when David and I were on our backyard court and our game of one-on-one was tied. It never got dark, there were no mosquitoes and I can't remember who won.

Did he go there too? That place free of suffering and despair that taunted me most mornings, that instant when it was 6:23 on that terrible autumn evening and it hadn't happened yet, where his skull hadn't been fractured despite his helmet's protection, where his blood hadn't poured out through his nose and ears onto the rough blacktop of the Rural Route we once drove past on the way to his Tom Thumb hockey games. Unlike Falkner's, this instant could not be summoned at mere command. It flits about my room in the space between dreams and cold reality, dissipating suddenly. Probably for my own good.

The young woman's knock and matter-of-fact greeting sent this mirage away, and I straightened up in my chair. The wall clock read a quarter to seven, and it was time for rounds. After the life-saving surgery the night of the accident followed by two weeks of skillful intensive care preventing his organs from shutting down, David's recovery had now stalled. After a surgery to return the piece of his skull to his head, a medical error caused another bleed, sending him back from the ability to produce short verbal responses and a first attempt to walk to nearly mute immobility. He was worse today than he was in November.

Furthermore, a C. difficile bacterial infection he acquired while in the hospital drained all of his remaining strength and had given him nearly a month of persistent diarrhea. Entering his room required putting on one of the assorted yellow smock gowns that were piled in a bin in front of the door, and some ill-fitting blue examination gloves.

The young woman was David's neurosurgery resident, and she gingerly pulled her arms through the sleeves of a yellow gown she picked up after she knocked. She was nice looking, with light brown hair and a professional appearance, perhaps my age or a year or two older. We introduced ourselves, and I quickly switched from comforter to advocate. This was the first doctor I had seen enter his room since I'd arrived five days earlier. She glanced at her chart and asked me a few questions about David's health, lightly gripping the toes of David's left foot with a gloved hand. David didn't respond to her questions, but his eyes followed her sleepily. I told the resident that we could also communicate with him with hand squeezes and yes-no questions, but she dismissed this idea by asking her next question.

In that instant I saw the workings of a profession I once idolized in a new light. For his resident, David was an obstacle on a hidebound tradition- rounds- that had been scrubbed of all of its prior utility. His resident was alone, busy and had other patients to see and notes to write. David wasn't 'her' patient. If David's value resided in his capacity to help her career- namely surgery stats- he was all but meaningless to her, and her demeanor gave that very impression. I asked her why the second bleed happened, why other precautions were not taken.

'Sometimes these things happen' was her terse reply. A few short, perfunctory questions later she was gone, draping the offending yellow gown over her arm as she pivoted on her heel and walked away.

Stunned, I looked at David. He stared straight ahead at the cards, pictures and exhortations sent from his hundreds of supporters that papered the facing wall. My face became flush with a brief spell of anger, which quickly morphed into indignation. I wanted to chase after her, to tell her about David, what he was like, who he was. I wanted to tell her about his gifts, about his creativity and charm. She'd only touched his foot. Did she see his value, his humanity? Could I make her understand? I remained motionless on the chair.

In the minutes that followed I sat next to David, holding his hand in mine. I refused to wear that glove. As his big brother I felt powerless to help, and although I wanted to scream, our shared silence was threatened only by distant beeps and the scuffle of hurrying feet in the hallway. He was broken, diminished, but his present incapacity did not define him- it was temporary, as the Spanish verb estar is to ser.

Looking at David, I resolved to do the best thing I could for him- I would remember. Memory is power. By actively recalling David- not merely his exploits on the playing field and his recent successes starting his career- but who he was: his smile, his quick wit and easy manner, his ability to dream without limitation. As we remembered these things, we would keep him alive. Not the 'him' that lay helpless in the bed but his ethereal counterpart- his identity, his soul- which

285

would return, one Sweet Day.

Today, in another –a better- hospital, our David is getting better.

I'm still remembering.

Taylor Raborn
May 24, 2012
Dear Team David:

This morning, on his last day at the Glenrose Hospital, David presents a $400 cheque to the Glenrose Physical Therapy Department, money that was raised from David's Bracket Challenge during the NCAA March Madness Tournament. With these funds the hospital will purchase new basketball and miscellaneous training equipment for patients to use during their rehabilitation.

Thank you to all of you who played, donating money to this worthy cause in David's name.

What a wonderful day!

Taylor Raborn
May 24, 2012
Dear Team David:
Today is a happy day. After 245 days of tears, heartache, separation, and anguish, our David leaves the hospital for good. He departs against all odds, has succeeded despite obstacles that we can scarcely comprehend. Last night he packed up his belongings, carefully placing them in bags that

286

he stacked next to the door. Among them are gifts you sent him from addresses all over the world: t-shirts, hats, jerseys and sweatsuits. Earlier, the cards and letters you sent him were taken down from the walls of his room, a display whose magnitude the nurses at both hospitals confided they'd never seen before. I'm his brother, but I'll probably never know what those tokens of love meant to him, and years from now these will hold more value to him than any material wealth in his possession. David's formidable inner strength enabled him to endure physical insults: walking when your legs are atrophied, the searing discomfort of four surgeries and one hundred and twenty stitches but also the mental kind: the incessant torment of self-doubt, the quiet horror of despair and isolation. As strong as David is, he would not be here without you. You helped him repulse the dark thoughts that arise when the mind is weakest. He may have been alone in his hospital room when they struck, but he was surrounded by the messages that represent your love for him. Even then, David was never alone.

You visited him in the hospital, arriving from points near and far to support him in his struggle. He doesn't remember every visit; during the fall and winter he was so sick his memories are hazy. But your presence brought him comfort, and the cumulative effect of seeing your kind faces and hearing your caring words gave him an inspired will to recover that not even the horror of his injury could withstand.

Before September, I had often read, and intellectually understood, that Love is the greatest force humankind has ever seen. After witnessing your support during the past eight months, this is now my most deeply held belief. You steadfastly refused to abandon a broken man, and with your help he is being made whole anew.

Along this winding path there are heroes that need to be mentioned, without any of whom this story would have taken a different turn. Running late to a hockey game, Bob Lloyd and his son stopped to help a bicyclist in distress. Bolstered by 16 years of medical training, the top neurosurgeon in Edmonton, Dr. Michael Chow, meticulously repaired the tears in David's brain vasculature overnight on September 22nd. His medical team at the neuroICU worked around the clock to keep him alive for three weeks as his organs threatened to shut down one by one. And when he arrived at the Glenrose Hospital in late February, the only patient in the unit fed through a tube, David was paired with a staff of doctors, nurses and therapists who never placed limits on his recovery.

Shortly after he entered through the doors of the largest rehabilitation hospital in North America, David's doctor privately feared that he would be confined to a motorized wheelchair for the rest of his life. In a few minutes, David will walk out of the Glenrose under his own power, never to return as an inpatient.

In early February I audaciously if less than confidently wrote that this would be 'David's Spring'. That is has been just that is a victory that we need to collectively cherish and celebrate. His journey to recovery has not ended, but as we help him climb back up the mountain let us pause, look out at the distance travelled, and be thankful. I love you David.

From the bottom of my heart, thank you.

David Raborn
August 2, 2012
Hey Everyone!

Thanks for being awesome and subscribing to my updates. I think it's time for a quick update from my end. Taylor just visited for a week so I'm incredibly blessed by that - thanks bud! I treasure your visit. Basketball was amazing. I wish you all were a fly on the wall when I met Taylor at the airport. It was amazing. To see his face in person after all these months. Wow!

Without your support and love, I know that I would not have made the gains that I have made. Your constant encouragement and visits while at the U of A hospital and the Glenrose will never be forgotten. I heard from the U of A hospital that no one received as many visitors as me. Thanks so much! You will all always be in my heart. Since leaving the Glenrose Hospital on May 24th as an outpatient I continue to return for rehab classes. Unfortunately, my favorite P.T presence at the Glenrose, Amanda, has moved to B.C. so I miss her. Other PT people have stepped up to assist my recovery. Additionally, I'm attending a sports class at the Glenrose once a week. My rehab will continue through the fall when I'll have a reassessment in late November. Driver retraining comes soon, as well.

I continue to work hard everyday - don't worry about that. As an example, we have a Bowflex machine and I work out 3-4 times a week on it and I walk 3 km a day.

Since leaving the Glenrose, my social activities have taken a definite turn for the better. Informal BBQs, birthdays, movies, fight nights, etc. Most importantly I've been able to attend worship at church, which has been helpful and meaningful. The congregations have been incredibly supportive during my ordeal.

For Taylor: I wanted to say how much your updates meant and will always mean to me. Thanks so much. To everyone: your postcards and messages have been incredible.

Most Sincerely,
David Raborn

Philippians 4:13

Taylor Raborn
February 20, 2013
Dear Team David:

Not too long ago I went to a stationary store. A small, well-decorated and locally owned place tucked away in the Arts District. My mission was to find cards I could send to a few of the people that had helped me earn my doctorate and to those who had given me graduation gifts. I wanted a certain type of thank you cards, the kind that are printed on a high-quality stock and have a particular scent that somehow makes me think of bookstores and groceries you carry in a paper bag. I browsed through shelves of cards- some with homemade features skillfully glued to the front, others with a gold leaf imprint. Their matching envelopes were fabricated in a manner that seemed to tell the recipient that there was to be an important message inside. These were special cards. And while I gazed through the inventory, my thoughts turned to The Accident, David's many months in the hospital and all of you. I thought about the acts of kindness, great and small, that you and many others performed during that dark period, and at my incapacity to adequately thank, let alone repay, each of you for doing them. I thought about the meals delivered to the hospital, the rides, the messages you sent, support of all kinds, and I came to the conclusion that I would not be able to truly repay you. For you, the most expensive, hand-crafted cards would not be sufficient.

Today is David's birthday. It's a happy day; a day that some doctors didn't think he would even reach. This year, unlike the last, he can stand up to blow out the candles on his birthday cake. This time he woke up in his own bed, and he'll be able to walk to the mailbox to pick up his gifts. Flying to Edmonton at this time last year, I watched David take his first steps in the Glenrose hallway- I could see in his eyes that he was determined to return to the people he loved and leave the hospital. For me, February 20th will always mean more than a birthday- it's a celebration of his life and of those-all of you- who supported him and us during our darkest hour. As I grow old with him, every February 20th will mean another year of victory over The Accident, a monument of love, medicine, kindness and unbreakable will that somehow put David and our family back together.

We were bound together by this horror, and we struggled our way out of the pit together. They don't make a card for what you did for us. Despite the fact that I'll never be able return the immense kindness you gave David and our family, please know that I am thankful for it and you. My heart is full and in this spirit I will endeavor to pass on similarly selfless deeds to others in the future.

Today, wherever you are, take a moment to celebrate David and our shared triumph. Think of his endurance and fortitude and the community we made when the landscape looked bleak and we dared not ponder the worst. Let's raise a toast to the strongest person I've ever met, his medical team and to the love that sustained us, together.
Happy Birthday, David. I love you.

Taylor Raborn
September 22, 2013
Dear Team David:

Two years ago this evening all of our lives changed as our David's hung in the balance. It's probably fitting that I write this during the evening hours, because it was during that time that the crisis unfolded: at the roadside, in the ambulance, at the Grey Nuns and finally at the University of Alberta Hospital.

As human beings we search for meaning in dates and symbols, and because of the gravity of what happened on this date two years ago September 22nd will always loom ominously on the calendar for me. I can recall every detail of that fateful Thursday, from the postcard I received from David to the flag football game I played while David's terrible accident took place. All of us learned about the accident differently, and I expect each of us responded to it in their own way, which a unique mixture of shock, sadness and disbelief. Ultimately my recollection is just one memory of the hundreds that comprise our collective Memory. I will share some of these remembrances.

I spent Thursday night and the early morning hours of Friday stricken in grief. At grave moments such as these our adrenaline wears off and only a dull feeling of horror remains. I gripped the postcard that had just been delivered and reread the photos and messages David had sent me minutes before he left on his bike ride.

The next day, as we realized how serious David's accident was, we made arrangements for me to fly home to see him in the hospital. David had gone through his second emergency surgery, this time to remove a large fraction of his skull. We now waited to see if David's condition would stabilize. In the hours that followed, his body's ability to maintain stability (a process called homeostasis), was no longer in place because of the swelling to his brain. Physiological processes that our bodies execute without any input from us were now replaced by nearly a dozen IV bags, which delivered drugs or solutes to his body. His organs, freed from the control of his hypothalamus inside his brain, now threatened to shut down. I spent Friday at home in Iowa City staring at a screen as a flimsy attempt to forget that my world was collapsing. The internist wasn't sure he would survive the night.

A certain natural order appeared to be upended that September evening. I thought about it as I boarded the 6AM flight from Cedar Rapids to Minneapolis, too numb to cry. I stared at the cornfields out my window and I considered this injustice. Older brothers don't bury brothers in their twenties during peacetime, I told myself, an axiom proven untrue all over the world. I'd seen David just three weeks prior at a close friend's wedding. He was the picture of youth and vitality, and I'd never seen him with such confidence. David was ready to make his way in the world. A part of me refused to believe the accident took place, the other was gripped with fury at the forces that allowed it to happen. I let myself consider the unthinkable, and I wondered what I would say at his funeral. This exercise ended when I couldn't envision myself saying that imagined eulogy without breaking down.

A friend drove me to the hospital from the airport, and he first thing I noticed when I arrived was how many people gathered in the waiting room. There were nearly fifty people in a space designed for fifteen. When I was ushered into the ICU my mother warned me that he didn't look like David. She was right, he didn't. This was shocking to others, too. A close friend of his had fainted a few hours earlier at the sight, dutifully removed from the ICU by a wheelchair.

The hours became days. I realized tearfully the following Monday that this wouldn't be a recovery that would be measured in weeks. Everyone had left for the night, back to their homes and families and jobs. The lights in the main atrium of the hospital were turned off and my cheerful façade dissipated.

We know how this story ends, with David sitting at home tonight, two years later, watching Sunday Night Football after a gathering with friends. Normalcy has slowly returned, and every milestone brings David closer to his life as it was

294

before the accident.

And yet nothing will ever be the same- we are all changed by these events, if only because we saw someone we love come infinitesimally close to death. Recalling the accident can sadden me in unexpected ways, and I find myself drawn to positive themes and people, avoiding harsh or hurtful words or sentiments.

We spend our lives fighting what physicists call entropy. Entropy is the tendency of nature to become more disordered over time, and it is an endless battle to stop or slow it. According to the Second Law of Thermodynamics, to reduce entropy requires the input of energy.

While David fought for his life and recovered from his accident, I observed a corollary to this Law. David and our family were broken physically and emotionally by this accident, it took not merely energy but love to put us all back together, to reduce the entropy the disaster had begotten.

It's impossible to estimate the number of gifts of love you provided to us, but we remember every one we possibly can. The fresh coffee brought to the waiting room, the transportation, the meals, visits, kind words, the help lent in a myriad of ways. I cannot imagine where our family would be without these expressions of love you provided so selflessly.

As a biologist I often think about how easy it is to disrupt something: a mutation in a key region of a gene can render an entire pathway or organism nonfunctional. It's vastly more difficult to confer a new feature or improve activity.

The same is true in our lives. A misplaced step can leave us bruised on the ground. A hurtful word can make us feel isolated and confused. To repair and undo these things costs much more than the forces that brought them about. But we must always spend our lives repairing, fixing, confronting those forces that do damage and tear apart. We do that with love. A stray pothole disrupted a speeding bike and its passenger that bright evening two years ago, and it brought me to my knees. It took the efforts of thousands to heal this tear in the fabric of the universe: A man and his son driving to a hockey game, who chose to stop and tend to a stranger on the side of the road. The neurosurgeon and his surgical team operating into the early hours of the night. The nurses who attended to all of David's needs for months, and the therapists who led him through his painful rehabilitation. The tissue that held it together was you: the support and love you provided to David and the kindness and dignity you provided to our family.

What I cannot repay to you I will hold in my heart for others. As I lead my life I do so with the knowledge that love is our only weapon against this ephemeral entropy: the tendency of things to fall apart. May we always recognize this power we have within us, and rejoice in the fact that despite the terrible accident that befell him two years ago, our David is still here with us, thriving.

That's something to smile about.

Taylor Raborn

January 12, 2014
Dear Team David:

Happy New Year! David and our family enter 2014 with more happiness and anticipation than we've had since before the accident. We hope that you had a warm and festive Holiday Season with you and your loved ones.

I spent a wonderful Christmas Holiday with David back in snowy Edmonton and wanted to share two poignant moments with all of you.

On Christmas Eve of 2012, David and I started a tradition of greeting the medical team in Unit 4A2 with festive donuts from Tim Hortons. This year we repeated the exercise, but with more donuts--three dozen this time, spread across both clinics and the waiting room-- and we brought our parents along. It was the first time that our mom had been in to the Hospital since February of 2012 when David left the U of A Hospital for good, and she told us that it was difficult to return because of the painful memories.
Every time he returns to 4A2, David is greeted like a rock star by the nurses and staff on duty, and this time was no different. Dressed up for Midnight Mass in a dark suit and gold tie, he was complimented repeatedly by the nurses, some of whom told him that they couldn't believe that this was the young man who just two years earlier required care around the clock. The staff sees many people enter the unit, but very rarely has the opportunity to see the benefit of their care and labour. David is a shining example to them as he is to us, a testament to the healing power of the meticulously crafted blend of scientific precision and humane arts that

297

comprises the best of Modern Medicine. We left together as a family after sharing our greetings and the team returned to work. We will return to thank them as long as we are in Edmonton, each year putting distance between us and the terrible Christmas of 2011.

It took some convincing, but David was finally permitted to do something he hadn't attempted since the accident: ice-skating. For those who don't know, David's first sporting love was hockey, and before the byzantine rules of minor hockey districting made it untenable, David was one of the top players in Northern Alberta in his age group.

We decided to make the trip to the Alberta Legislature rink, and the lightly falling snow and falling temperatures made it a perfect setting for what was to come. We hiked across the grounds, and before I could get my laces tied in the locker room, David was already on the ice. David would be the first to tell you he hasn't yet reached his pre-accident levels of foot speed and agility, but on the ice he was a perfect picture of swiftness, grace and power. It was reminiscent of the time only a handful of years earlier when he was asked to play a game of shinny hockey with some of our mutual friends at Millennium Place, all former Midget AAA or AA players. David, who had switched from hockey to basketball and football at age 12, was in his element even in this talented group.

For 45 minutes he glided across the ice, darting in every direction as the younger skaters, and later a few members of a bachelorette party, admired his skill. This was small and wondrous sign- another barrier that no longer exists for

David. It was amazing in its ordinariness- hundreds of thousands of such scenes dot the Canadian landscape every winter, and we were just one of them; David's mastery of this skill belying nothing of the painful journey he had made to get there. David was nonplussed by my happiness: "I knew I could do it, it's not a big deal" was the essence of his comments afterward as we trudged through the snow back to the vehicle.

And therein lies the paradox inherent in every milestone David achieves. Each of them are themselves victories, but in many ways they are inevitable, the battle already having been won. Viewing them in isolation, the wonder of each of these milestones can fill me with emotion. But to David they are just part of his return to normalcy, something that we fuss about but he just sees as part of his life. I'm conflicted by this- it is human nature that the routineness of each of David's achievements will eventually condition us to cheer less frequently at their occurrence.

For a moment I stopped skating and stood at the edge of the rink, tracking David's agile movements with my eyes. The other skaters, the trees and river valley behind him blurred as I brought David into sharp relief. My heart became full as I recognized the meaning and magic of the scene. David is no longer a patient, someone with a sliver of hope to whom things are done, IVs are inserted, procedures administered to. Today David is doing things: dreaming dreams, making plans, living his life. There is a beauty in this that I never want to become immune or resistant to. That cold day, and as I recount it today, I chose to see the Magic.

What we are seeing unfold represents the best in all of us, something each of you have contributed to. As the extraordinary becomes ordinary for David, let us all catch a glimpse of that Magic again, if only for a moment.

-Taylor

Appendix

Brain Trauma, Concussion, and Coma

Peter M. Black, Patricio C. Gargollo, and Adam C. Lipson, The Dana Foundation

Head trauma and the resulting brain injuries are one of the leading causes of death and disability in the industrialized world. In the United States, more than 50,000 people die every year as a result of traumatic brain injury. Furthermore, it is estimated that a head injury occurs every seven seconds, and hospital emergency rooms treat 1 million people for brain injuries every year. Currently about 5.3 million Americans — a little more than 2 percent of the U.S. population — live with disabilities resulting from such injuries.

Traumatic brain injury may occur at any age, but the peak incidence is among people between the ages of 15 and 24. Men are affected three to four times more often than women. Motor vehicle accidents are the leading cause, accounting for approximately 50 percent of all cases. Falls produce the most brain injuries in people older than 60 and younger than 5. Other causes include violent assault and firearms misuse. It has been estimated that after one brain injury, the risk of a second injury is three times greater, and that after a second injury, the risk of a third is eight times greater.

There are many head injury symptoms, ranging in seriousness. Minor injuries will cause mild or no symptoms, while severe injuries will cause major derangement of function. The most common symptom of brain injury after head trauma is a disturbance of consciousness; some people remain awake, but others are confused, disoriented, or unconscious. Headache, nausea, and vomiting are other common symptoms.

Anyone who sustains a head injury should be examined by a physician. Symptoms of brain trauma can be initially subtle, seemingly unrelated to the head, and not immediately apparent. A person who has sustained a serious head injury should not be manipulated or moved by people who are not trained to do so, because this may aggravate an injury.

Diagnosing Brain Trauma

The first thing doctors do when assessing a head injury is determine whether the person is in imminent danger of death. Once the person's vital functions are stabilized, physicians examine the individual from a neurological perspective, checking:

- level of consciousness
- function of the cranial nerves (through pupillary responses to light, eye movements, and facial symmetry)
- motor function (strength, symmetry, and any abnormality of movements)

- breathing rate and pattern (linked to brain stem function)
- deep tendon reflexes, such as the knee jerk
- sensory function, such as response to a pinprick
- external signs of trauma, fracture, deformity, and bruising in the head and neck

Each of these parts of the physical exam will give a physician clues about the extent and location of any brain injury.

Doctors also need to know about the person's behavior before, during, and after the injury. All of these points yield clues about what might have happened and how best to treat the person. Family members or people who witnessed the accident can usually provide helpful information. They can help medical professionals provide the best care possible by taking note of certain symptoms:

- unusual sleepiness or difficulty awakening
- mental confusion
- convulsions
- vomiting that continues or worsens
- restlessness or agitation that continues or worsens
- stiff neck
- unequal pupil size or peculiar eye movements
- inability to move arms and legs on either side
- clear or bloody drainage from the ears or nose
- bruising around the eyes or behind the ears
- difficulty breathing

This is a partial list.

Physicians can use a variety of radiological tests to assess a person with head trauma. Most hospital emergency departments can now do computed tomography (CT) scans. CT provides more information, and is excellent for diagnosing skull fractures, bleeding, or other important lesions in the brain. CT also helps doctors follow people with head trauma as they recover. Magnetic resonance imaging (MRI) currently has little involvement in diagnosing and treating an emergency, but once a person's condition is stable an MRI may provide useful information that a CT cannot, such as evidence of white matter damage.

Different types of injuries require particular treatments. Surgery is needed to remove blood or foreign material, or to reconstruct parts of the skull. Very often brain trauma causes tissue to swell against the inflexible bone. In these cases, a neurosurgeon may relieve the pressure inside the skull by placing a ventriculostomy drain that removes cerebrospinal fluid. If the swelling is massive, a neurosurgeon may remove a piece of the skull so that the brain has room to expand; the surgeon keeps and reimplants the bone after the swelling has gone down significantly. Often during these procedures, the surgeon places a small pressure valve inside the skull to measure pressure on a moment-to-moment basis.

Most nonsurgical management of brain trauma involves close monitoring, often in an intensive care unit, to prevent further injury. Physicians will conduct further neurological exams in order to assess whether the person is improving or worsening. Doctors have no "miracle drug" to prevent nerve injury or improve brain function immediately after trauma, but they can use medication to modify a person's blood pressure, optimize the delivery of oxygen to the brain tissue, and prevent further brain swelling.

Specific Injuries in Head Trauma

Trauma to the head can produce many problems because so many components may be injured. Brain tissue is surrounded both by the skull and by a tough membrane called the dura, which is right next to the brain. Within, and surrounding, the brain tissue and dura are many arteries, veins, and important nerves (the cranial nerves). Therefore, trauma to the head may damage the skull, the blood vessels, the nerves, the brain tissue itself, or all of the above. Depending on the nature and severity of their injuries, people may exhibit a very wide range of symptoms: from absolutely none to coma.

Injuries to the Skull

Fractures of the skull can be divided into linear fractures, depressed fractures, and compound fractures. Linear fractures are simple "cracks" in the skull. Most require no treatment. The concern with these fractures is that a force large enough to break the skull may have damaged the underlying brain or blood vessels. This is especially true for fractures of the bottom, or "base," of the skull.

Depressed skull fractures are those in which part of the bone presses on or into the brain. The extent of the damage depends on what part of the brain the depressed skull overlies, as well as the nature of any associated injuries to other tissues.

In compound fractures, the trauma is severe enough to break the skin, bone, and dura and expose the brain tissue. These types of fractures are usually associated with severe brain damage.

Treating skull fractures depends on the extent of damage to structures beneath the bone. Most linear fractures will not damage other structures unless the fractured bone becomes displaced and presses on the brain. In this case a surgical repair may be necessary to restore the bone to its normal position. Depressed skull fractures are usually also treated surgically in order to restore normal anatomy and prevent damage to underlying tissues by bone fragments.

Compound fractures are a special case since, by definition, there has been contact between the brain tissue and the outside air. These fractures therefore bring the possibility of infection from environmental debris. The fracture site is therefore vigorously cleaned and decontaminated before repair. In addition, these fractures are usually associated with severe injuries to the brain, blood vessels, and nerves, and repairing these structures may also be necessary.

Injuries Involving Vessels

Injuries to the blood vessels within the skull may lead to the collecting of blood in abnormal places. A collection of blood outside a vessel is called a hematoma. In all of the following types of hematomas, individuals are in danger if there is enough accumulating blood to press on the brain or other important structures within the skull. (In this respect, a head injury can resemble a hemorrhagic stroke.) In these cases, the hematoma may compress the brain and shift it from its normal position. Too much shifting can damage the crucial brain stem. Bleeding may also raise the pressure inside the skull to the point that it shuts off the blood supply to the brain (as in an ischemic stroke. These conditions can be very serious and require emergency surgery.

- **Epidural hematomas** occur between the skull and the dura. These are usually caused by a direct impact injury that causes a forceful deformity of the skull. Eighty percent are associated with skull fractures across an artery called the middle meningeal artery. Because arteries bleed quickly, this type of injury can cause significant bleeding within the skull and require emergency surgery. Although uncommon (affecting only 0.5 percent of all head-injured individuals), epidural hematomas are a surgical emergency, and people with this type of injury must have the damage immediately repaired in the operating room.

- **Subdural hematomas** appear between the dura and the surface of the brain. These are more common than epidural hematomas, occurring in about 30 percent of people with severe head trauma. They are produced by the rupture of small veins, so the bleeding is much slower than in epidural hematomas. A person with a subdural may have no immediate symptoms. As blood slowly collects within the skull, however, it compresses the brain and increases the intracranial pressure.

There are three types: acute, subacute, and chronic. The acute subdural may cause drowsiness or coma within a few hours and requires urgent treatment. A subacute subdural should be removed within one to two weeks. The most treacherous is a chronic subdural hematoma. It is not uncommon for such an injury to go undiagnosed for several weeks because individuals or their families do not recognize subtle symptoms. A person may appear well but nonetheless have a large subdural. That is why it is important for a heath professional to evaluate all individuals with head injuries. Depending on the symptoms and size of the subdural, treatment may involve careful monitoring or surgical removal of the blood.

Scans should be done on any person with prolonged headaches or other symptoms after head injury.

- **Intracerebral hematoma**. Injuries to small blood vessels in the brain may also lead to bleeding within the brain tissue, called an intracerebral hematoma. The effect of this hematoma depends on how much blood collects, and where, and whether the bleeding continues. Doctors may respond conservatively, finding no need for treatment, or treat the problem as an emergency. More than half of people with intracerebral hematomas lose consciousness at the time of injury. There may be associated brain contusions with this hematoma.

- **Subarachnoid hemorrhage**. Bleeding may occur in a thin layer immediately surrounding the brain (the subarachnoid space). In head trauma, it is common to have some degree of subarachnoid hemorrhage, depending on the force applied to the head. In fact, subarachnoid hemorrhage is the most commonly diagnosed abnormality after head trauma. CT detects it in 44 percent of severe head trauma cases. Fortunately, individuals with subarachnoid hemorrhage but no other associated injuries usually do very well. However, they may get delayed hydrocephalus as a result of blockage of the flow of cerebrospinal fluid.

Injuries to the Brain Tissue

Our brains are somewhat mobile inside our skulls, which can give rise to other injuries. There are some spiny

309

contours on the inside of the skull, but under normal circumstances a barrier of cerebrospinal fluid surrounds the brain and cushions it from direct contact with the hard bone. However, when a person's head is subjected to violent forces, the brain may be forcibly rotated and battered within the skull. During such episodes brain tissue may be ripped, stretched, battered, and bruised. Bleeding, swelling, and further bruising of brain tissue usually follows. In these cases, people usually sustain permanent damage.

Injuries to the brain are classified according to the degree of tissue damage that they cause. It is important to remember that the different types of brain injuries are part of a spectrum. There may not be a clear distinction in every case, and one person may suffer multiple types of injuries.

Concussion. A concussion is a temporary and fully reversible loss of brain function caused by direct injury to the brain. It is the mildest form of brain injury, usually resulting from minor trauma to the head. In concussions, it is not possible to identify any structural damage to the brain tissue.

Contusion. Contusions are localized areas of "bruising" of the brain tissue. They consist of areas of swollen brain and blood that has leaked out of small arteries, veins, or capillaries. Contusions will often occur under the impact point on the skull (coup). They may also, in the same incident, occur on the side directly opposite the impact because the brain may rock away from the blow and strike the inside of the skull (contrecoup). Sometimes the skull is broken at the site of a contusion, but not always. Whatever the cause, contusions are likely to be most severe in the tips of the frontal and temporal lobes, after trauma forces these areas of the brain against bony ridges inside the skull.

Lacerations. Lacerations are actual tears in the brain tissue. They can be caused by shear forces placed on the brain, or by an object (such as a bullet) penetrating the skull and brain. The degree of damage depends on the depth and location of the laceration, as well as on whether associated blood vessels and cranial nerves suffer damage.

Diffuse axonal injury. Diffuse axonal injury (DAI) refers to impaired function and eventual loss of axons (the long extensions of nerve cells, which enable them to communicate with one another). It is caused by the acceleration, deceleration, and rotation of the head during trauma, as in a car crash, probably the most frequent cause of this type of injury. These forces can stretch and shear axons. DAI is a microscopic injury that does not show up on a CT scan. Therefore, diagnosing DAI depends on physicians' observations. Individuals with this sort of injury are usually unconscious for longer than six hours and, depending on the degree and location of axonal injury, may remain this way for days or weeks. DAI may be mild and reversible or, if extensive, may lead to severe brain damage or death. This is the most common cause of injury from high-velocity trauma and has no treatment.

Brain swelling and ischemia. Often, a person's immediate injury may not be the worst. Usually, there is additional secondary injury to the brain that occurs hours to days later. The damage to the brain tissue, blood vessels, and nerves causes the brain to swell. If that swelling is severe, the blood supply to the brain may be blocked (ischemia), leading to tissue death. Also, since the brain is encased in a hard skull, the swelling may actually compress the tissue against bone. Excessive compression of areas such as the brain stem, which is responsible for regulating our breathing and consciousness (among other vital functions), can lead to severe disability and death.

Long-Term Outcome

Perhaps the most widely used system to predict outcome after head injury is the Glasgow Coma Scale (GCS). The individual is evaluated in each of three parameters, and the sum of the three parts provides the total score.

People with mild head injury, usually defined as Glasgow Coma Score 13–15, tend to do very well. These individuals have often suffered concussions or minor degrees of brain swelling or contusion. Although headaches, dizziness, irritability, or similar symptoms may sometimes trouble them, most suffer no residual effects. For people with a simple concussion, the mortality rate is zero. Of people with mild brain swelling, fewer than 2 percent die.

People with moderate head injuries (GCS 9–12) do less well. Approximately 60 percent will make a good recovery, and another 25 percent or so will have moderate degrees of disability. Death or persistent vegetative state (PVS) will be the outcome for 7 percent to 10 percent. The remainder are usually left with severe disability.

People with severe head injuries (GCS under 8) have the worst prognoses. About 25 percent to 30 percent of these individuals have good long-term outcomes, 17 percent have moderate to severe disabilities, and 30 percent die. A small percentage remain in PVS.

In penetrating head injuries, such as those inflicted by bullets, the statistics are a bit different. Over half of all people with gunshot wounds to the head who are alive when they arrive at a hospital later die because their initial injuries are so severe. But the other half, with more mild injuries, usually do fairly well.

The outcome for people in coma after brain injury depends in part on their age. People under 20 are three times more likely to survive than those over 60. One study found that people who showed no motor response to painful stimuli and no pupillary response to light (normally our pupils get smaller when light is shone on them) 24 hours after brain injury were likely to die. However, the presence of both of these responses was a very positive finding, especially in young people.

Rehabilitation After Brain Injury

People who have suffered head trauma and resultant brain injury will often benefit from some physical therapy during their hospital stay or after they leave the hospital. If they are not acutely ill, moving to a rehabilitation program may speed any further recovery. These centers usually teach individuals strategies for reaching the maximum level of functioning their impairments allow. People sometimes have to relearn skills essential for everyday activities. Another major goal of these centers is to work with families to educate them about realistic future expectations and how they can best help their injured family member.

After brain trauma, individuals may have persistent cognitive or emotional disabilities that include:

- short-term memory loss
- long-term memory loss
- slowed ability to process information
- trouble concentrating or paying attention for periods of time
- difficulty keeping up with a conversation
- problems finding words
- spatial disorientation
- organizational problems and impaired judgment
- inability to do more than one thing at a time

Physical consequences can include:

- seizures
- muscle weakness or spasticity
- double vision or impaired vision
- loss of smell or taste
- speech impairments such as slow or slurred speech
- headaches or migraines
- fatigue, increased need for sleep
- balance problems

Long-term recovery from brain injuries depends on many factors, including the severity of the trauma, associated injuries, and a person's age. Unlike in the movies, people rarely recover their preinjury level of functioning after severe head trauma. Rather than emphasizing complete recovery, treatment aims to improve function, prevent further injury, and rehabilitate individuals and their families physically and emotionally.

Black, P.M., Gargollo, P.C., & Lipson, A.C. "Brain Trauma, Concussion, and Coma." In *The Dana guide to brain health: a practical family reference from medical experts.* Edited by F.E. Bloom, M.F. Beal, & D.J. Kupfer. New York: Dana, 2006.

Made in the USA
Columbia, SC
12 October 2017